D1234167

The purpose of this study guide is to provide supplemental educational material. It is not intended as a substitute for or replacement of the original source text.

Published by SuperSummary, www.supersummary.com

ISBN: 9798445736837

For more information or to learn about our complete library of study guides, please visit http://www.supersummary.com.

Please submit comments or questions to: http://www.supersummary.com/support/

Table of Contents

Overview

Twenty Thousand Leagues Under the Sea is a science fiction adventure novel by French author Jules Verne. It was originally published in serialized form in 1869 under the title *Vingt mille lieues sous les mers*, and later as a book in 1870. In 1873, the first English-language translation was released. The book was highly acclaimed at the time of its publication and was one of several successful novels by Verne. Others include *Journey to the Center of the Earth*, *From the Earth to the Moon*, and *Around the World in Eighty Days*—all of which are also in the science fiction and adventure genres. Along with his other novels, *Twenty Thousand Leagues Under the Sea* brought Verne great wealth and fame. Several film adaptations of the book were made in the 20th century, including a highly successful version produced by Walt Disney in 1954. The book remains a literary classic and continues to be one of the most translated works of fiction in the world.

Plot Summary

Frenchman Pierre Aronnax, professor of natural history and his loyal servant Conseil join Commander Farragut and his crew aboard the *Abraham Lincoln*. Their mission is to find and destroy a giant sea monster that has been attacking ships around the world. While the *Abraham Lincoln* is in close pursuit, it collides with the creature, sending Professor Aronnax into the water. Conseil jumps in to rescue him. Clinging to the creature, they find Canadian harpooner Ned Land, who had also been on board the *Abraham Lincoln*. The three men realize the monster is not a living creature, but a submarine made of iron. They soon gain entrance after banging on the exterior walls of the ship before it descends under the water.

Once inside the ship, the men are ushered into a cabin, where they are made to wait before being introduced to the ship's commander, Captain Nemo—a pseudonym that means "no one." Captain Nemo tells them that they are prisoners, although they are free to do what they please around his vessel, a submersible ship called the *Nautilus*. This ship is a secret, and to let them go risks it being found out. Captain Nemo then gives Professor Aronnax a tour of the *Nautilus*, which is a marvel of advanced engineering and design. Powered by electricity, it travels at great speeds and depths. Captain Nemo explains that food, fuel, and other resources all come from the sea.

Professor Aronnax, Ned, and Conseil commence their journey with Captain Nemo, exploring the world under water. They are exposed to dozens of different sea creatures and plants, and taken on submarine excursions using an advanced diving apparatus devised by Captain Nemo. On one such excursion, Captain Nemo leads Professor Aronnax to the lost civilization of Atlantis, showing him ancient ruins at the bottom of the sea. On another, Captain Nemo saves a humble pearl diver from sharks and gifts the stranger a bag of pearls. Nemo tells Professor Aronnax that he is always on the side of the oppressed, with whom he identifies. They also explore the far reaches of the globe, even reaching the South Pole, which Captain Nemo has claimed in his own name. Professor Aronnax feels admiration and respect for his captor, and expands his studies of the subsurface environment.

However, Professor Aronnax knows their status as prisoners is unsustainable, particularly as Ned is anxious to regain his freedom. They are also keen to unravel the mystery of Captain Nemo's past, especially after Professor Aronnax must examine a fatally injured crewmember after he, Ned, and Conseil are drugged and forced to spend the night locked in a cabin. As they travel, Nemo becomes quieter and more withdrawn, increasingly obsessed with pushing the boundaries of exploration and seeking revenge. He massacres dozens of cachalots, or sperm whales, which earns him the further ire of Ned—who considers this poor hunting form. On their excursion back from Antarctica, they are all nearly suffocated when the *Nautilus* becomes trapped in underwater ice. Later, they battle giant poulps, or octopuses, one of whom kills a crewmember.

As a result of Captain Nemo's dark turn, Professor Aronnax sees him in a different light. He feels nostalgia for land and empathizes more deeply with Ned's desire to escape. When Captain Nemo mercilessly sinks a vessel that attacked them, Professor Aronnax knows that the man he once respected has become overwhelmed by hate. As the *Nautilus* approaches a violent maelstrom, Professor Aronnax, Ned, and Conseil escape to the small boat attached to the ship. As the *Nautilus* is sucked into the whirlpool, a reflection of Captain Nemo's rage, the small boat is flung out of danger and the three men arrive safely on land, finally earning their liberation. While Captain Nemo's fate remains unknown, Professor Aronnax hopes that his hate has been conquered by his quest for knowledge and desire to explore and understand the depths of the sea.

Chapter Summaries & Analyses

Part 1, Chapters 1-9

Part 1, Chapter 1 Summary: "A Shifting Reef"

In the middle of the 19th century, many of those who travel the sea have caught sight of a large, fast-traveling object in the water. Although estimates of its size vary, it is clearly bigger than any sea-faring creature in existence.

Ships begin to encounter the moving object directly in July 1866. They note its incredible speed—one ship sees it in the Pacific Ocean three days after another saw it five miles off the Australian coast. As other ships also see the "monster" (2), witnesses speculate that it is more than 350 feet in size.

The monster becomes "the fashion" (2)—in cafés, newspapers, and the theater. It is caricatured, satirized, sung about, and compared to the mythical creatures of ancient cultures. Debates rage between "incredulous" (3) scientists and those who believe in the supernatural. By early 1867, however, the entity is viewed as an immediate danger—possibly a type of reef or rock to be avoided.

In spring of 1867, two ships strike what seems to be a rock. The impact leaves a large hole in the bottom of the ships. When engineers in Liverpool examine it, they note that the hole is a perfectly defined isosceles triangle. After piercing the ship, the object pulled away in a "retrograde motion" (5) that is impossible to explain. The public once again goes into a frenzy; authorities decide that all 200 ships that recently disappeared at sea were lost because of the monster.

Part 1, Chapter 2 Summary: "Pro and Con"

Professor Pierre Aronnax now becomes the novel's narrator.

The mysterious monster in the water attacks happen as Aronnax prepares to return home to Paris in May 1867. As an Assistant Professor in the Museum of Natural History in Paris, he has been in the territory of Nebraska in the United States for research. He has been following reports about the mysterious sea object. There are two opinions about what it might be: a monster with great strength or a submarine "of enormous motive power" (6). However, such a machine seems technologically impossible. Governments have denied building it, and it is difficult to imagine a private citizen building something like this without detection.

In New York, Professor Aronnax is asked his opinion about the situation— a result of having previously published a well-respected book on submarines called "Mysteries of the Great Submarine Grounds" (6). In an article published in the *New York Herald,* he argues that the object must be a creature of the sea. The paper quotes him as saying it may be something as yet unidentified that has risen from the lower levels of the ocean, or an abnormally large "unicorn of the sea" (7), or a narwhal. Narwhals have big, iron-like tusks that can do incredible damage; one with "colossal dimensions" (8) could potentially penetrate a ship. Public opinion favors Professor Aronnax's view.

In New York, the ship *Abraham Lincoln* is prepared for an expedition to pursue the monster under Commander Farragut. Three hours before the ship is scheduled to leave, Professor Aronnax receives a message from the United States Government asking him to join the expedition.

Part 1, Chapter 3 Summary: "I Form My Resolution"

Although Professor Aronnax longs to go home to Paris, he suddenly feels that pursuing the monster is his true calling. He usually travels with his dutiful Flemish servant of 10 years, Conseil, without asking whether Conseil wants to join him, even when the voyage may be long and "hazardous" (10). Professor Aronnax tells Conseil to gather everything together for the trip—they are going in search of the monster.

They arrive at the ship and meet Commander Farragut. Professor Aronnax observes that the *Abraham Lincoln* is "a frigate of great speed" (11). As the ship departs, he realizes how close he came to missing this "extraordinary, supernatural, and incredible expedition" (11). The ship is escorted by several boats and cheered on by thousands of people until it heads away from the coast of Long Island and into "the dark waters of the Atlantic" (12).

Part 1, Chapter 4 Summary: "Ned Land"

According to Professor Aronnax, Commander Farragut is the "soul" (12) of the ship—a fitting captain for the *Abraham Lincoln*. Farragut unquestionably believes in the existence of the sea monster and has made it his mission to kill the creature or die trying. The other officers on the *Abraham Lincoln* share Captain Farragut's opinion and daily watch from the rigging for a sign of the monster. Farragut has offered a reward of $2,000 for the first person to spot it.

The ship is well equipped to catch a narwhal. It is armed with an arsenal of weapons. Also on board is a Canadian harpooner named Ned Land, an imposing man who "knew no equal in his dangerous occupation" (13). The natural bond between Canadians and the French leads Ned to gravitate toward Professor Aronnax, who listens to Ned's tales of the polar seas. The two also bond over the dangers they now face together.

Ned is the only person on board who doesn't believe in the monster. His doubt stems from experience: He does not know of any cetaceans that could penetrate the iron plates of a ship. Professor Aronnax argues that such a creature is possible: It would have "incalculable strength" (15) to survive the pressures of the ocean's depths, since the deeper one goes into the ocean, the more pressure the water exerts on the body. At 32,000 feet, the pressure is a crushing 97,500,000 pounds. If the monster can bear this, it must be powerful enough to pierce a hull.

Part 1, Chapter 5 Summary: "At a Venture"

During the trip, Ned briefly boards another ship to help them catch a whale. Instead of catching one, he catches two and impresses everyone with his "dexterity" (17). On July 6th, the *Abraham Lincoln* sails around Cape Horn, at the tip of South America—a decision made by Commander Farragut to avoid passing through the narrow Straits of Magellan. They then enter the waters of the Pacific.

Professor Aronnax spends all of his time on the poop deck, watching the water. Every time a sea creature is spotted, everyone gathers in excitement, but it usually only turns out to be a whale. They stay away from land and sail in deep water—where the monster has often been spotted. They live in a perpetual and "violent" (18) state of excitement as the ship explores the Japanese and American coasts.

Although they do not want to give up, Captain Farragut makes the decision on November 2nd to turn around if the monster is not spotted within three days. Everyone rallies to get the narwhal's attention. They throw bacon in the water and circle the *Abraham Lincoln* in small ships. On the night of November 4th, Ned shouts that he's spotted "the very thing we are looking for" (20).

Part 1, Chapter 6 Summary: "At Full Steam"

Ned is pointing at an object that gives off light of an "electrical nature" (21) and seems to be rapidly heading toward them. Captain Farragut tells Professor Aronnax he thinks the creature is an electric narwhal and he needs to wait until daylight to attack it, since he is not sure of the proper defense against the animal.

All night, everyone aboard can hear the strokes of its tail and "panting breath" (23). They prepare to hunt the creature, but are met with an intense fog in the morning. As the fog lifts, Ned spots the creature again and Professor Aronnax notes that its size was exaggerated, estimating that it is only around 250 feet long. As it releases water shooting upward to 120 feet, he concludes it is a mammal.

Captain Farragut gives the orders to go full steam ahead toward the animal, but no matter how fast they go, it manages to stay ahead of them at speeds Professor Aronnax estimates to be nearly 30 miles per hour. Captain Farragut orders the gunners to shoot at it, vowing that he will "pursue that beast till my frigate bursts up" (25). A gunner manages to hit the creature, but the shot isn't fatal. After several hours, the animal still shows no signs of slowing down.

As night falls, the electric light once again reappears. Professor Aronnax assumes that the animal must be resting. Captain Farragut takes the opportunity to once again try to attack the creature. This time, they get close enough for Ned to strike. His harpoon hits what sounds like a "hard body" (26). Suddenly, the light goes out and the creature collides with the ship. Professor Aronnax is tossed overboard.

Part 1, Chapter 7 Summary: "An Unknown Species of Whale"

Professor Aronnax quickly swims to the surface, gets his bearings, and sees that the *Abraham Lincoln* is sailing away from him. He feels himself slipping into the ocean when Conseil suddenly grabs him—he jumped into the water to save his master. While Professor Aronnax is panicking, Conseil remains calm.

In order to preserve their strength, the men alternate between resting and swimming. They determine their best chance is to wait for one of the *Abraham Lincoln's* boats to pick them up. However, soon Aronnax is overcome with fatigue. He despairs when he spots the *Abraham Lincoln* five miles away.

Just when Professor Aronnax begins to sink into the water from exhaustion, Conseil's cries for help are suddenly met with a response. Something pulls them up out of the water—it's Ned, who fell into the water as well, but was able to catch himself on the entity they were pursuing. It's not a narwhal, but is something made of iron. Professor Aronnax realizes that this "natural phenomenon" (30) is actually a man-made vessel.

The machine starts to move and they all grab hold tightly. Ned tells them they are fine unless the machine dives. Professor Aronnax searches for a way in and wonders what lurks inside of the craft. In the morning, Ned kicks at the wall of the vessel, shouting to be let in. Suddenly, an iron plate moves and a man appears. He gives an "odd cry" (31), and then eight men wearing masks bring Ned, Conseil, and Professor Aronnax inside.

Part 1, Chapter 8 Summary: "Mobiles in Mobili"

Inside, the men find themselves in total darkness in a small cabin. Suddenly, a bright light comes on, which Professor Aronnax recognizes as the same electric light that they mistook for phosphorescence. The source of the light is a "half globe" (32) in the cabin's roof.

The cabin contains only a table and stools. Suddenly, a door opens, and two strangers enter the room. One has dark hair, a thick mustache, and the physiognomy of people from the South of France. The other is, according to Professor Aronnax, "the most admirable specimen I had ever met" (33). He appears self-confident, calm, energetic, and courageous, yet his hands suggest "a highly nervous temperament" (33). The two men speak in an unfamiliar language. Professor Aronnax and Ned talk to them in French, English, German, and Latin, but they have no success.

The two men leave, and Ned yells in frustration that they will starve to death. Professor Aronnax reminds him they have suffered through worse and surmises that the two men are southern; however, whether they are "Spaniards, Turks Arabians, or Indians" (34) remains unclear. A steward brings them a change of clothes in an unfamiliar fabric, sets the table, and brings in food—a meal worthy of a world class hotel featuring many kinds of fish. Each utensil is engraved with the letter "N" and the motto "Mobilis in Mobili" (35). After finishing their meal, they are overcome with fatigue. Professor Aronnax is initially distracted by anxious thoughts and nightmares, but eventually relaxes and succumbs to sleep.

Part 1, Chapter 9 Summary: "Ned Land's Tempers"

Professor Aronnax wakes fully rested. The table has been cleared, but otherwise, the cabin is unchanged. He notices that the air feels heavy; as soon as he wonders how the air supply will be replenished, he feels a burst of fresh air enter the cabin and notes a ventilator above the cabin door. He determines from the motion of the boat that they have just gone up to the water's surface to breathe.

The burst of fresh air wakes Conseil and Ned, who wonders what time it is. They are hungry and the steward has not returned with more food. Ned grows impatient and angry as two more hours pass. He starts to shout, but there are no sounds outside the cabin. Eventually, the steward enters and Ned lunges at him, gripping him around the throat. As Conseil and Professor Aronnax prepare to intervene, the ship's commander enters. He addresses them in French as "Master Land" and "Professor" (38) and asks them to listen to him.

Part 1, Chapters 1-9 Analysis

The mystery surrounding the *Nautilus* introduces the book's theme of technological innovation. Even a learned man like Professor Aronnax concedes that the ocean, a vastly unexplored part of the globe, could conceivably house enormous narwhals, giant sea creatures, or similar members of "the vertebrate branch, class mammalia" (24) that humans have yet to discover. Alongside the crew of the *Abraham Lincoln*, he undertakes a hunt that hearkens to large-creature narratives like Herman Melville's 1851 novel *Moby Dick* or the big game hunting memoir genre popular in the 19th century. However, the novel then veers away from the natural world and into the brand new genre of science fiction, positing the existence of a powerful and fast submersible ship. Although experiments with this kind of "human construction" (30) had been going on in the real world, no 19th-century submersible could match the imagined potency of Verne's invention. Interestingly, France did create the world's first functional submarine in 1804—named, coincidentally enough, *Nautilus*—though Verne actually used a different vessel, the French Navy ship *Plongeur*, as a model for Captain Nemo's sub.

As narrator Professor Aronnax, Conseil, and Ned make their way inside the submarine, the air of mystery that initially surrounded the ship is transposed onto its captain. Even when Captain Nemo makes his first appearance, his personality remains elusive, and his identity as the ship's commander is not yet revealed. The trio stranded on the *Nautilus* find themselves completely disoriented: They are confused about how much time has elapsed, seemingly unable to communicate with their captors, fed at stressfully irregular intervals, and even concerned about the availability of fresh air. All of this heightens the sense that the life they knew and understood has given way to a whole new reality. The transition is marked at the end of Chapter 9, as Professor Aronnax feels the boat sinking and experiences "Dreadful nightmares" of "a world of unknown animals, amongst which this submarine boat seemed to be of the same kind" (35-36). His dreams prefigure experiences yet to come.

Part 1, Chapters 10-23

Part 1, Chapter 10 Summary: "The Man of the Seas"

The man speaking to them is the ship's commander. He tells them in French that although he speaks French, English, German, and Latin, he has cut ties with humanity. Professor Aronnax interjects that their meeting him was unintentional, but the man scoffs—the *Abraham Lincoln's* pursuit was hardly unintentional. Professor Aronnax responds that the whole world has been talking about his ship, and that they were chasing what they thought was a dangerous monster.

The commander believes he has a right to treat them as enemies, insisting that he would have been well within his rights to let them drown. Professor Aronnax argues that only a savage, not a civilized man, would do this—to which the commander responds that he is not a civilized man. He no longer obeys society's laws. However, he will allow them to remain on board as free men, as long as they submit to being in their cabins when he commands: They are his "prisoners of war" (41) as they have discovered the secret of his existence.

The man introduces himself as Captain Nemo and his vessel as the *Nautilus.* Captain Nemo then takes them to eat breakfast in an opulent dining room. They are served food that once again seems to be only from the sea. Captain Nemo explains that it is the only food he and his crew eat. Captain Nemo loves the sea because the violent reign of man does not exist below the water's surface. It is the only place where true independence and freedom lie.

Captain Nemo shows Professor Aronnax around the ship: a library fit for a palace, which contains 12,000 books; and a drawing room that is like a "magnificent museum" (46), which contains "all the treasures of nature and art" (45), Nemo's "last souvenirs of that world which is dead to me" (46). Professor Aronnax expresses his admiration for the collection and the ship itself. He hopes to understand how the *Nautilus* works. Captain

Nemo will show him, but first takes him to an elegant bedroom—
Professor Aronnax's new quarters. This room adjoins Captain Nemo's,
which by contrast is "severe, almost monkish" (48).

Part 1, Chapter 11 Summary: "All by Electricity"

Captain Nemo shows Professor Aronnax several familiar nautical
instruments on the walls of his room: a thermometer, barometer,
hygrometer, storm-glass, compass, sextant, chronometers, and glasses.
These tell Nemo the ship's position and direction. There are also
instruments with which Professor Aronnax is not familiar. Captain Nemo
reveals that they are powered by electricity. Professor Aronnax doesn't
understand how this is possible: How could such a fast-moving ship can
be powered by a source whose "dynamic force has remained under
restraint, and has only been able to produce a small amount of power"
(49)? Captain Nemo uses sodium extracted from the ocean water to
produce the electricity needed for heat, light, and motion on the *Nautilus*.
Some of the equipment on the walls measuring time and speed is also
powered by electricity.

Captain Nemo next takes Aronnax to the ship's stern. The 150-foot long
back part of the boat includes the dining room, library, drawing-room, the
Captain's room, Professor Aronnax's room, and a reservoir of air. Water-
tight partitions separate the rooms and contain doors that seal
hermetically in case of a leak. In the middle of the ship, a ladder leads to
a small boat inside a water-tight cavity. They then pass a kitchen
powered by electricity rather than gas, a bathroom, the crew's berth-
room follows, and finally the large engine-room. The engine-room is
divided into two parts. One part includes the materials needed to
produce electricity; the second, the machinery that connects to the first
part with a screw. The engine can perform 120 revolutions per second,
which results in a speed of 50 miles per hour.

Part 1, Chapter 12 Summary: "Some Figures"

In the saloon, Captain Nemo shows Professor Aronnax a sketch of the
Nautilus. The ship is shaped like a cigar, measuring 232 feet in length, 26
feet in width, and weighing 1500 tons. Its strength is the result of two
steel-plated hulls and dives when Nemo fills its reservoirs with water

based on precise calculations. When Professor Aronnax wonders how the ship withstands water pressure when diving, Captain Nemo responds that he uses inclined planes on the sides of the ship to slowly travel down diagonally. A steersman in a thick glass box above the hull uses lenses to steer. An electric reflector behind the box provides light for half a mile in front of the ship. Professor Aronnax yells "bravo" (55) with excitement and realizes this light accounts for what they all mistook as phosphorescence.

The *Nautilus* is a perfect vessel, and Nemo loves it "as if it were part of myself" (55). He is the ship's builder and engineer, as well as its captain; he constructed it in secret by bringing in parts separately from all around the world to a deserted island. Professor Aronnax asks Captain Nemo if he is wealthy, to which Captain Nemo replies that he is "Immensely rich, sir" (56).

Part 1, Chapter 13 Summary: "The Black River"

Over 80 million acres of water cover the earth's surface. The Earth was initially all water; when land formed, it separated the water into the Arctic, Antarctic, Indian, Atlantic, and Pacific Oceans. The Pacific is the "quietest" (57) of the oceans and is where the *Nautilus* is currently. The ship ascends to the surface and Professor Aronnax goes outside to the platform, which stands three feet above the water. The outer surface of the ship is comprised of overlapping iron plates that could easily be mistaken for the shell of an animal.

Captain Nemo provides the ship's course and maps for Professor Aronnax. The ship is to follow the Black River, moving from the Gulf of Bengal into the North Pacific. Ned and Conseil enter the room. Professor Aronnax encourages them to take in the marvels around them, but Ned insists they are in a prison. The lights go out and two iron panels open up, revealing crystal-plated windows that look into the water all around them, illuminated by electric light. Ned temporarily forgets his anger and they watch for two hours as an "aquatic army" (60) escorts the ship, in awe of the vast array of ocean life that surrounds them.

Part 1, Chapter 14 Summary: "A Note of Innovation"

Professor Aronnax awakes the next morning, November 9. He passes the time studying some of the mollusk shells and dried herbs. Captain Nemo does not appear. The next day, Ned and Conseil join Professor Aronnax and wonder at the captain's absence. On November 11, Professor Aronnax observes that they are back at the water's surface. He goes back up to the platform to take in the fresh air. Captain Nemo's second in command appears, scans the horizon, and says four words that Professor Aronnax does not understand.

Five days continue the same way. Finally, Professor Aronnax gets a letter from Captain Nemo inviting him, Conseil, and Ned hunting on the island of Crespo. On the planisphere, a kind of globe, they find the island—a small rock in the North Pacific. On November 17th, Professor Aronnax finds Captain Nemo waiting for him in the saloon. They will be hunting in a submarine forest using a version of the Rouquayrol apparatus—a reference to a real diving suit designed by inventor Benoît Rouquayrol in 1862. It allows them to roam free from the ship by storing air in an iron knapsack with two rubber pipes—one to exhale and one to breathe in fresh air and a copper helmet to mitigate pressure. A Ruhmkorff lamp—the work of another real-world inventor, Heinrich Daniel Ruhmkorff—is used for illumination. Captain Nemo explains that they will hunt with an air gun which uses electricity instead of gunpowder.

Part 1, Chapter 15 Summary: "A Walk on the Bottom of the Sea"

Ned expresses disappointment that the hunt will be underwater and refuses to put on the heavy rubber diving gear required. Conseil, Captain Nemo, and Professor Aronnax suit up in india-rubber clothes, boots, and gloves. With Professor Aronnax's approval, they put on their helmets, which allow them to see in all directions through three glass holes. They put Rouquayrol breathing apparatuses on their backs and hang Ruhmkorff lamps from their belts. They are pushed into a small room and a water-tight door is sealed. Another door opens and they are suddenly walking on the ocean floor.

Captain Nemo takes the lead. Professor Aronnax feels weightless, and notes that, with the solar lamps, he can see up to 150 yards in front of him. The water is transparent, and it is as though they are "in broad daylight" (68). They see a kaleidoscope of colors reflecting off the objects in front of them: coral, fungi, anemones, sea-stars, phsyalides, pelagiae, medusae, and mollusks. The sandy ground gives way to mud, followed by a luxurious bed of sea-weed. Captain Nemo points to a dark mass "looming in the shadow" (70). It is the submarine forest.

Part 1, Chapter 16 Summary: "A Submarine Forest"

The forest contains a variety of large, straight, perpendicular plants. They walk, observing the colorful plant and sea life. Unable to speak to one another, Professor Aronnax puts his helmet to Conseil's and sees his eyes "glistening with delight" (71). They walk for another four hours before Professor Aronnax is overcome with fatigue and falls asleep.

Professor Aronnax wakes up and the sight of a giant sea spider brings him quickly to his feet in terror. Captain Nemo shoots it with his gun and it falls over in convulsions. Professor Aronnax decides he needs to be more alert, as larger, more predatory creatures may be lurking. In the darkness, Captain Nemo puts on his light and everyone follows. After four hours, they reach a wall of steep rocks. Since they cannot scale it, they turn around and walk back to the ship. The walk back seems steep and different from the way they came. Just as Professor Aronnax thinks they have not encountered anything worth shooting, Captain Nemo shoots a rare sea otter with valuable-looking fur. Captain Nemo's companion slings the otter over his shoulder and they keep walking.

A sandbar brings them close to the surface, where Captain Nemo kills a large albatross hovering above them. When they see the light of the *Nautilus* ahead, Professor Aronnax feels his oxygen is depleting. Just then, Captain Nemo quickly pulls him to the ground—there are two sharks swimming above them, but the "Monstrous brutes" (74) pass over them without incident due to their poor eyesight. Back on the *Nautilus*, Professor Aronnax retreats to his room in "great wonder at this surprising excursion at the bottom of the sea" (75).

Part 1, Chapter 17 Summary: "Four Thousand Leagues Under the Pacific"

The day after the submarine forest hunt, Professor Aronnax returns to the ship's platform where Captain Nemo is taking some "astronomical observations" (75). Several sailors come out to catch fish in nets—men of European descent who use the strange language spoken by Captain Nemo's second in command. They bring in hundreds of fish of "infinite variety" (76).

Captain Nemo tells Aronnax that the sea has a "pulse, arteries, spasms" (76), and a circulation not unlike the way blood circulates through the body. Nemo envisions a future of "independent" (76) submarine towns. Wound up, Nemo angrily mentions a "despot" (76)—ostensibly something from his past—but quickly changes the subject to the depth of the ocean. Professor Aronnax thinks that its deepest point, the South Atlantic, is 15,000 yards deep. Captain Nemo hopes to show Professor Aronnax that it is deeper than that.

Over the course of the next weeks, the ship continues to head southeast. They pass Hawaii in late November and cross the equator on December 1. They encounter a shoal of millions of calmars—a type of squid studied by the ancients and enjoyed as a dish for the wealthy. The calmars swim with the ship for hours and the nets bring in a large number. On December 11, Conseil spots a black mass out the window—a sunken ship resting perpendicular in the water. It has been wrecked for only a few hours, providing a "sad spectacle as it lay lost under the waves" (79). They spot six corpses on the bridge—four men and a woman holding an infant. The *Nautilus* turns away just as sharks appear. Professor Aronnax catches sight of the ship's name: *"The Florida, Sunderland"* (79).

Part 1, Chapter 18 Summary: "Vanikoro"

The sighting of the shipwreck is the start of a "series of maritime catastrophes" (79) for the *Nautilus*. Professor Aronnax studies the enormous walls off the Island of Clermont produced by a variety of corals that take hundreds of years to be raised. The ship switches direction, sailing West North West, and passing Tahiti. Ned Land expresses disappointment that they are not celebrating Christmas. On December 27, Captain Nemo joins them in the dining room after having been absent for a week. He tells Professor Aronnax they are at the Vanikoro islands, the site of the lost expedition of French explorer Lapérouse—a real French naval officer and explorer.

Aronnax lays out the historically accurate details. In 1785, King Louis XVI sent Lapérouse on an expedition with two ships, the *Astrolabe* and the *Boussole*. The expedition was never heard from again. In 1824, Captain Dillon of the *St. Patrick* found debris from the ships. He returned in 1827 to investigate further, gathered a number of relics, and returned to France. However, at the same time, Commander Dumont d'Urville went to Vanikoro in another ship named the *Astrolabe*. He was told that a third boat, constructed by castaways, had also been lost. No one knows where the third boat perished.

Captain Nemo adds details of the story: One ship was destroyed immediately, while the other lay stranded. The castaways were welcomed by the natives and decided to make a smaller boat out of debris from the other two. Some of the castaways stayed on the island, while others headed out with Lapérouse toward the Solomon Isles. However, that ship was also wrecked at sea. Professor Aronnax wonders how Captain Nemo came about this information. Captain Nemo shows him a tin box that he found at the wreck containing instructions from the naval minister to Lapérouse, with annotations written by Louis XVI himself.

Part 1, Chapter 19 Summary: "Torres Straits"

The *Nautilus* leaves Vanikoro with "great speed" (85). On January 1, Conseil wishes Professor Aronnax a happy New Year, explaining that a happy year is one "in which we could see everything" (86). Captain Nemo's plan is to get to the Indian Ocean by passing through the Strait of Torres, a difficult route due to a number of obstacles like islands and rocks. Professor Aronnax, Ned, and Conseil go up to the platform to watch the ship navigate the Straits. Despite the dangerous course in front of them, the *Nautilus* glides "like magic off these rocks" (87).

However, near the Island of Bilboa, the ship runs into some rocks. There is no damage to the ship, but it becomes stuck. Captain Nemo insists that the full moon in five days will raise the tides enough to move the

Nautilus. Ned thinks the tide will most likely not budge the ship, and he argues that they should abandon the *Nautilus* since they are near the island of New Guinea. The captives are surprised when Nemo grants them permission to temporarily visit the island.

Part 1, Chapter 20 Summary: "A Few Days on Land"

Professor Aronnax, Ned, and Conseil finally find themselves on dry land again, two months since becoming prisoners of the *Nautilus.* Ned beats down "cocoa-nuts" (91) from a tree, and the three men enjoy them and wonder if they might bring some on board the ship. Conseil suggests they bring fruits, vegetables, and venison. In the dense forest that covers the island, they find a bread-fruit tree, and Ned makes bread-fruit pie, a "delicate pastry" Professor Aronnax eats "with great relish" (92). They continue through the forest, gathering cabbage-palms, beans, and yams to bring them back to the boat.

The next day, they head to a different part of the island, letting Ned take the lead. They hunt some of the many birds they see; Conseil shoots down two pigeons for breakfast. Ned will not be happy until he eats game that is four-footed. Professor Aronnax would like to catch a bird of paradise, so Conseil catches one that is drunk from eating nutmegs. Ned then brings down a hog, followed by several small "kangaroo rabbits" (95). They enjoy a feast for dinner on the shore. When Conseil suggests they spend the night away from the *Nautilus,* Ned suggests they never go back. A stone suddenly falls at their feet.

Part 1, Chapter 21 Summary: "Captain Nemo's Thunderbolt"

When another stone knocks a pigeon's leg from Conseil's hand, the three men make a run for the boat. A hundred Native people aggressively enter the water behind them. Back on the *Nautilus,* Professor Aronnax tells Captain Nemo with urgency about the "Savages" (97) ready to attack, but Captain Nemo reassures him that the *Nautilus* can withstand it. With his fears eased, Professor Aronnax begins to appreciate the "splendours of the night in the topics" (97). The next morning, he returns to the platform to see several hundred Indigenous on the shore. He recognizes them as Papuans.

Professor Aronnax decides to fish with Conseil. After two hours, Professor Aronnax excitedly pulls out a shell from his net—an olive porphyry that spirals from left to right, rather than the usual right to left, which makes it very valuable. Just then, a Native man throws a stone at the shell and breaks it. Conseil shoots him with his gun, knocking a bracelet off the man's arm. Professor Aronnax yells at Conseil, arguing that the shell is not worth the man's life. As the Indigenous shoot arrows in response, Professor Aronnax runs into the ship and tells Captain Nemo they are under attack. Captain Nemo calmly replies they must close all the ship's hatches.

The *Nautilus* is currently near the spot where Dumont d'Urville nearly wrecked his ship. Captain Nemo rues this famed explorer's unfortunate death in a railway derailment, his emotion on the subject giving Professor Aronnax "a better opinion of him" (101). Together, they chart the explorer's travels; Captain Nemo compares d'Urville's land expeditions to his own in the sea—which he claims to have done with more detail and ease.

The next morning, the tide shifts the *Nautilus* against the rocks. As they open the hatches to depart, the Native people try to get in, but a nonfatal electric shock from a metallic cable prevents them.

Part 1, Chapter 22 Summary: "Aegri Somnia"

The *Nautilus* continues its journey going at least 35 miles per hour. Because the ship so easily—and nonlethally—deterred the natives, Professor Aronnax feels "unbounded" (104) admiration for the ship and its captain.

The days continue to pass and life "seemed easy and natural" (106) until an event reminds them of the lives they left behind. On January 18, a storm makes the sea rough. Captain Nemo exchanges words with his lieutenant, who seems to be in a state of agitation. They begin pointing at something, but when Professor Aronnax gets out his telescope to see what they are looking at, Captain Nemo angrily snatches it from him. He asks Professor Aronnax to honor his promise to go to his quarters until Captain Nemo releases him.

As soon as Professor Aronnax relays the message to Ned and Conseil, the three men are taken to the cabin from their first days on board the ship. The lights go out in the room and Ned and Conseil quickly fall into a heavy sleep. Professor Aronnax suspects they have been given something to sleep with their food, because he is also unable to keep his eyes open. He succumbs "to a morbid sleep, full of hallucinations" followed by "complete insensibility" (109).

Part 1, Chapter 23 Summary: "The Coral Kingdom"

The next day Professor Aronnax wakes up back in his room. Ned and Conseil also woke up back in their own cabins. The ship seems as "quiet and mysterious as ever" (109). Captain Nemo, looking fatigued, suddenly asks Professor Aronnax if he is a doctor—he needs help with one of his men. Professor Aronnax was a resident surgeon at a hospital before working at the museum.

In another cabin, an injured man lies in bandages covered in blood. Professor Aronnax removes the bandages, exposing a large head wound. The man will not live more than a couple of hours, which brings tears to Captain Nemo's eyes. After watching the dying man for a few minutes longer, Captain Nemo dismisses Professor Aronnax. The scene haunts Aronnax and he does not sleep well.

The next morning, Captain Nemo asks Professor Aronnax on another "submarine excursion" (111). Professor Aronnax asks to bring Ned and Conseil, and the men suit up and head out into a coral reef with Captain Nemo and some of his companions. This coral is particularly valuable and could make them a fortune. After two hours they are 300 yards deep, and the seascape begins to change into a forest of mineral vegetations and petrified trees. Captain Nemo and his men are carrying an oblong object. They stop at a cross made of coral and one of the men begins to dig a hole. Professor Aronnax realizes they are in a cemetery, digging a grave to bury the man who died in the night. They lower his body—the oblong object—into the grave, cover it, and then kneel and extend their hands in a farewell salute. Back on the ship platform, Captain Nemo tries unsuccessfully to "suppress a sob" (114) and remarks that the man is not forgotten.

Part 1, Chapters 10-23 Analysis

The novel explores the theme of civilization and what it means to be a civilized person. As Professor Aronnax gets more acquainted with Captain Nemo, he does his best to understand his captor's nature. Captain Nemo's priceless collection of art, artifacts, books, music, and objects from the sea seems to point to a highly educated man who appreciates the highest achievements of European civilization. However, at the same time, Captain Nemo lives in a "world apart" (60), forging his own reality and turning his back on humanity with contempt for its tyrants. Nemo's dreams of a series of independent submersible cities points to his disdain for civilization as Europeans know it; his humane treatment of the Native people attacking the Nautilus contrasts with France's approach to suppressing its colonial subjects around the world. Similarly, although Professor Aronnax, Ned, and Conseil are prisoners, Captain Nemo keeps them in comfortable and even luxurious quarters; moreover, Nemo seems eager to make sure that their captivity is intellectually and emotionally enriching, promising that Professor Aronnax will "not regret the time passed" (42) on the *Nautilus* and will "visit the land of marvels" (42).

The novel displays the broad research that Verne conducted before writing, featuring complex explanation of technologies like the submarine's electricity-powered navigational tools and a variety of diving gear that enables Captain Nemo to conduct underwater hunts. Verne's references to real-life inventions, and his extrapolation that when perfected, these would be able to sustain the kind of adventure he is describing, are all hallmarks of the science fiction genre to this day. Similarly, Verne describes the marine life around the ship with zoological precision, making sure to note the ship's passage around the world with accuracy and to match the fauna they encounter with their geographical position. This attention to minute detail is a feature of all of Verne's adventure novels, and it is all the more remarkable given that Verne never traveled outside of France himself, basing his writing on the firsthand accounts of others.

Professor Aronnax is riveted by his captor and the mystery surrounding him, especially the more he sees Captain Nemo's humane side. When Captain Nemo asks Professor Aronnax to help with a dying crewmember, Captain Nemo is in an unrecognizable state of "violent agitation that pervaded his whole frame" (107)—a depth of emotion that contrasts with his typically cool and collected demeanor. There is clearly a larger conflict going on, though Nemo prevents his prisoners from learning about it by making them spend a night locked in the cabin and drugged into sleep. The moving ceremony of the underwater burial of the dead crewmember suggests that Captain Nemo's embrace of innovation and exploration masks a darker truth.

Part 2, Chapters 1-11

Part 2, Chapter 1 Summary: "The Indian Ocean"

Conseil decides that Captain Nemo is a "misunderstood genius" (115) who has sought refuge in the sea where he can do what he pleases without being disturbed. Professor Aronnax agrees that this is part of his personality, but having seen Captain Nemo's anger and despair, views him as a man seeking revenge.

On January 24, they are in the Indian Ocean heading west. Professor Aronnax passes his time studying the ocean, reading books in the library, and writing his memoirs. They see many aquatic birds, including albatrosses, sea-swallows, and phaeton, and a variety of fish unique to the Indian Ocean that Professor Aronnax has never seen before. They pass Keeling Island, a site visited by Charles Darwin, and then head northwest.

On January 25, Conseil and Professor Aronnax watch hundreds of argonauts—mollusks who travel backward—traveling along the water's surface until they suddenly all disperse from a "sudden fright" (119). The next day, the *Nautilus* crosses the equator into the northern hemisphere, escorted by several varieties of sharks. They encounter dead bodies from an Indian village floating on the water. That night, they sail into a "milk sea" (120), where the water is white from a luminous worm that can stretch for dozens of miles.

Part 2, Chapter 2 Summary: "A Novel Proposal of Captain Nemo's"

On January 28, the *Nautilus* surfaces and Professor Aronnax spots the Island of Ceylon. Captain Nemo asks Professor Aronnax if he would like to see one of the Island's pearl fisheries on the Bank of Manaar. Captain Nemo notes that they will also be armed to hunt sharks. Professor

Aronnax begins to sweat at the thought when Ned and Conseil enter. They have seen Captain Nemo and know about the fishing excursion, but nothing has been mentioned to them about the sharks.

Professor Aronnax explains to Ned and Conseil that pearls are jewels that come from oysters. The fisherman extracts them either with pincers or by boiling the oyster's tissue and separating the pearls through a sieve. The pearls are priced according to shape, color, and brightness. Ned wonders at the risks of such a profession, to which Professor Aronnax responds by asking Ned if he's afraid of sharks. Ned scoffs at the question. Conseil says if Professor Aronnax is prepared to face the sharks, then so is he.

Part 2, Chapter 3 Summary: "A Pearl of Ten Millions"

The next morning, Nemo's men slowly row Professor Aronnax, Ned, Conseil, and Captain Nemo under a dark sky. As they get close to land, the boat drops anchor and they get into their diving gear. Everyone is armed with a dagger, and Ned also has a giant harpoon. They walk into the water until they disappear under the waves.

At seven in the morning, they reach the oyster banks. They enter a dark grotto embedded in rocks. Professor Aronnax sees an enormous oyster that he guesses to be 600 pounds. Captain Nemo opens the oyster's shell with his dagger to expose a large loose pearl of "inestimable value" (128). Professor Aronnax reaches out to grab it, but Captain Nemo stops him—he is allowing the pearl to continue to grow.

As they hide behind rocks, a fisherman dives from his canoe with a stone between his feet, filling up his bag with oysters when he reaches the bottom of the water. He then resurfaces, dumps the bag in his boat and dives down again. Suddenly, the fisherman gets a look of terror in his face as a shark charges him. It knocks the man to the ground with its tail, preparing to strike. Captain Nemo moves toward the shark, stabs it several times with his dagger, but is unable to kill it. Professor Aronnax can only watch, "nailed to the spot in horror" (129).

As the shark rushes toward Captain Nemo, Ned kills it with his harpoon. Captain Nemo grabs the fisherman and rushes to the surface where Captain Nemo and Conseil successfully resuscitate the man. Captain Nemo hands the man a bag of pearls, and he takes it with "a trembling hand" (130). When they reach the boat, Captain Nemo thanks Ned.

Professor Aronnax concludes from the excursion that Captain Nemo has "unparalleled courage" (131) and is capable of kindness to another person. Captain Nemo says the man is from an oppressed country—the same one where Captain Nemo was born.

Part 2, Chapter 4 Summary: "The Red Sea"

The *Nautilus* has traveled 7,500 leagues, or 16,220 miles, since they started their journey in the Japanese Seas. For the next few days, they sail around the Sea of Oman, without seeming to have a clear destination.

They sail along the Arabian Coast into the Red Sea. There are thousands of species of fish, as well as zoophytes, mollusks, and reptiles. Captain Nemo asks how Professor Aronnax is enjoying the Red Sea. Professor Aronnax responds positively. The two men agree that the *Nautilus* is a century before its time.

Captain Nemo reveals that he has been in the Red Sea before. Professor Aronnax asks if he's seen any evidence of where Moses parted the sea for the passage of the Israelites, as described in the Book of Exodus from the Bible's Old Testament. Captain Nemo has not, but only because that particular spot is "blocked up with sand" (136). Captain Nemo predicts that future excavations will reveal "arms and instruments of Egyptian origin" (136). Professor Aronnax hopes this will happen soon, before the completed Suez Canal brings forth new towns on the isthmus. Captain Nemo praises the work of Ferdinand de Lesseps, the Frenchman who is responsible for the development of the Canal—adding that he brings honor to the French nation.

However, they will not be traveling through the Canal. They are instead going to the Mediterranean via a passage under the isthmus—the "Arabian Tunnel" (138). Nemo discovered it by deducing that identical fish in the Red Sea and the Mediterranean meant that there must be a "'subterranean current'" (138) between the two.

Part 2, Chapter 5 Summary: "The Arabian Tunnel"

On February 10, Professor Aronnax joins Ned and Conseil on the platform. Suddenly, Ned points to a spot on the water less than a mile away. They determine it's an animal and Captain Nemo gives Ned his approval to take the smaller boat and kill it, warning him not to miss or the creature might overturn the boat. Seven crew members suddenly appear and lower the smaller boat into the water. Professor Aronnax, Ned, and Conseil take their seats near the back.

Professor Aronnax watches the creature, which he identifies as a "colossal" (141) halicore dugong. It looks like a manatee and has an oblong body with a long tail, and two pointed teeth in its upper jaw. Ned prepares to harpoon it. He strikes and injures the creature, but does not kill it. The dugong barrels toward the boat, diving beneath the water each time Ned attempts to strike it. After an hour of chasing the dugong, the animal finally throws itself onto the boat. The boat fills with water and the situation is chaotic until Ned strikes the creature in the heart, killing it. They return to the *Nautilus* and hoist it onto the platform with great effort, since Professor Aronnax estimates it weighs 10,000 pounds.

The next day, the *Nautilus* passes Mount Horeb, where, according to the Torah, Moses saw God. Later that evening, they are near the Suez Canal. Captain Nemo assures Professor Aronnax they will be entering the Arabian Tunnel soon and enters the steersman's cage—a small cabin measuring "six feet square" (143)—to navigate the difficult path ahead. Professor Aronnax watches from the port-scuttle, noting the strong pilot who holds the wheel. The ship follows a high wall, the base of "a massive sandy coast" (143). They enter a large opening, and Captain Nemo guides them into the Mediterranean.

Part 2, Chapter 6 Summary: "The Grecian Archipelago"

Ned tells Conseil and Professor Aronnax that since they are near Europe, he wants to leave the *Nautilus*. Professor Aronnax has no desire to do so —he would like to see where the journey goes. Professor Aronnax is not sure if he would take his freedom if Captain Nemo offered it to him. Ned thinks they should take the first opportunity to leave the ship. They will only get one "favourable opportunity" (146), and Captain Nemo will never forgive them if he catches them. If the ship comes close enough to the European coast, Ned has decided to swim for it. Otherwise, he'll take the small boat. Professor Aronnax doesn't think the opportunity to escape will ever occur because Captain Nemo knows they still desire their freedom and will be vigilant. As they sail around the Mediterranean, the *Nautilus* stays mostly underwater and far from land.

In the evening, Captain Nemo joins him in the saloon and opens the panels, looking out "attentively" (147). Suddenly, Professor Aronnax sees a diver in the water. He yells to Captain Nemo it is a man who has been shipwrecked and must be saved. Captain Nemo explains it is a well-known diver named Nicholas of Cape Matapan. He then walks over to a chest and opens it to display "an enormous sum" (149) of gold ingots. He writes an address on the chest and summons his crew, who push the chest out of the saloon and hoist it up using pulleys.

Professor Aronnax tries to draw a connection between the diver and the chest of gold. He hears the *Nautilus* going up to the surface, the small boat being lowered into the water, and then returned to its socket two hours later. The next morning, he tells Conseil and Ned everything that transpired. Later, in the saloon, Professor Aronnax is overcome by the heat—they are in the boiling water near the Island of Santorini. The saloon soon becomes too hot to bear and Captain Nemo orders the ship to move. Professor Aronnax realizes if they had chosen that region for their escape, they never would have made it out alive.

Part 2, Chapter 7 Summary: "The Mediterranean in Forty-Eight Hours"

They travel through the Mediterranean in 48 hours. When Captain Nemo does not appear, Professor Aronnax realizes it is because he is surrounded by countries he wants to avoid. Their rapid pace of travel also means Ned has to abandon his escape plans. Launching the small boat with the *Nautilus* traveling at 25 miles per hour would be like "jumping from a train going at full speed" (152).

As the ship passes between Sicily and Tunis, it slows down considerably to navigate a high reef that joins Europe and Africa. Conseil wonders if a volcano will raise the two barriers up over the surface of the waves. Professor Aronnax reassures him that it is unlikely because volcanoes are not as active as they were in "the first days of the world" (154); now, the earth is in a process of cooling and will one day no longer be inhabitable. That day, however, is still hundreds of thousands of years away. Before the ship dives back down, they observe sponges, outspread phosphorescent sea-cucumbers, and comatulae.

Part 2, Chapter 8 Summary: "Vigo Bay"

They reach the Atlantic, which Professor Aronnax heralds as a "Magnificent field of water" (156) that is 9,000 miles long and covers 25 million square miles. Ned plans to escape that night, since they will be near the Spanish coast. He has gathered some provisions in the boat. Professor Aronnax can wait in the library for his signal. Professor Aronnax counters that the water is too rough, but Ned believes liberty is worth the price. As the hour approaches to leave, Aronnax feels intense anxiety, mostly worrying that Captain Nemo will be sad at their departure. He goes to the saloon to look at Nemo's collection one last time. He is abandoning forever "These wonders of Nature, these masterpieces of Art" (158).

When it's close to nine, Aronnax heads to the library to wait for Ned's signal. Captain Nemo enters, and proceeds to tell him the history of Spain, starting in 1702, when Louis XIV placed his grandson, Phillip V, in charge of the Spaniards. An alliance between Holland, Austria, and England desired instead to place Charles III on the throne. Spain needed to resist the coalition, but did not have soldiers or sailors. However, they had wealth in the form of gold and silver from America, which was coming via a fleet commanded by Admiral Château-Renaud. The Spanish wanted the fleet to enter Vigo Bay, a Spanish port, but this left them defenseless. The English soon arrived. Although Spain managed to offload some of the treasure, Admiral Château-Renaud sent the remaining riches to the bottom of the ocean, rather than let them fall into enemy hands. Captain Nemo announces that the sunken treasure is still in Vigo Bay.

Professor Aronnax sees through the windows several divers carrying to the *Nautilus* cases of gold, silver, and jewels. Captain Nemo is the "heir direct, without any one to share, in those treasures torn from the Incas" (161). Captain Nemo points out that he can pick up such treasures anywhere in the world. It is the source of his millions. When Professor Aronnax asks whether Nemo feels bad that "thousands of unfortunates" (162) are deprived of such riches, Captain Nemo argues that he does not gather the riches for himself only, and that he is not ignorant of the sufferings of oppressed people around the world.

Part 2, Chapter 9 Summary: "A Vanished Continent"

When Ned confronts Professor Aronnax about their failed escape mission, Professor Aronnax tells Ned about the treasures that Captain Nemo and his men were collecting at Vigo Bay. Ned hopes they may be able to try again that night, but when Professor Aronnax checks the compass, he sees they are heading away from Europe. While Ned is angry, Professor Aronnax feels some relief.

Later that night, Captain Nemo asks Professor Aronnax if he wants to join him on a submarine walk at night. Professor Aronnax agrees and they suit up. No one else is joining them, and they leave their lamps behind. They head to the bottom of the Atlantic, their way guided by a bright red light shining two miles away. Professor Aronnax's eyes adjust to the darkness and he hears rain falling on the surface of the water. They head away from the *Nautilus* and toward the bright, rosy light. As they get closer, Professor Aronnax realizes the light is a reflection of a fire on the other side of the mountain. He feels confident they won't get lost, viewing Captain Nemo as "a genie of the sea" (165).

To get up the mountain, they have to first travel over rocks and through groups of dead trees. Professor Aronnax feels no fatigue, and notes that Captain Nemo doesn't either. Two hours later, they finish walking through the trees and see the mountain rising a hundred feet up. Professor Aronnax sees the ruins of castles and temples built in Tuscan architecture. Captain Nemo traces the word "ATLANTIS" (168) in chalk on a rock. Professor Aronnax is in awe of the ruins of "the buried continent" (169). Captain Nemo finally turns and gestures to Professor Aronnax to follow. They reach the *Nautilus* as the first light of dawn appears.

Part 2, Chapter 10 Summary: "The Submarine Coal-Mines"

A few days later, Professor Aronnax sees only darkness out the window. He's confused, expecting daylight. Captain Nemo explains that they are floating underground—they are on a lake in the "heart of an extinct volcano" (171), a place of refuge from all severe weather. There is a crater at the top to supply air and a coal mine to provide coal for the electricity on the ship. Captain Nemo's men extract the coal in their diving suits. Captain Nemo invites Professor Aronnax to spend the day exploring.

Professor Aronnax finds Ned and Conseil and takes them to the platform. Ned is frustrated that they are once again on land, but beneath a mountain. They walk around, and Professor Aronnax observes vegetation on the sides of the mountain: euphorbia, heliotropes, chrysanthemums, and violets, which he stops to smell. Ned excitedly identifies a beehive in a dragon-tree. He obtains several pounds of honey by lighting his flint and smoking out the bees. He looks forward to using it to make a cake. Professor Aronnax also spots birds of prey. Ned kills one with a rock and puts it in his bag, along with the honey. They head back down to the shore and onto the ship, which does not immediately depart—Captain Nemo is waiting until nightfall when they can leave undetected.

Part 2, Chapter 11 Summary: "The Sargasso Sea"

The next day, they reach the Sargasso Sea, "a perfect lake in the open Atlantic" (175). The ship stays beneath the waves to avoid the carpet of seaweed on the surface, a phenomenon explained by the circular movement of the Gulf Stream in the Atlantic around a central point. Many things float in the seaweed, including tree trunks and debris from wrecked ships. There are also pink halcyons, actiniae, and medusae.

For the next 19 days, as the *Nautilus* sails around the Atlantic, Ned worries they will have no opportunity to escape. Professor Aronnax wonders if they might be able to persuade Captain Nemo to let them leave and "restore our liberty" (176) if they promise never to tell anyone of their experiences, as Captain Nemo made it clear that he requires their lifelong imprisonment to keep his existence a secret.

The *Nautilus* descends lower than 7,000 fathoms, despite the pressure on the ship. They reach a depth of 4 leagues, losing sight of all animal life, and withstanding a pressure of 1600 atmospheres. Professor Aronnax is filled with excitement at experiencing the ocean's unexplored depths. He wishes he had some way of remembering it—something Captain Nemo says is possible. He has his men bring in equipment to take a negative through the open panel, which captures primitive rocks, granite, and a "horizon of mountains" (178). He then tells Professor Aronnax to hold on because they must rapidly ascend, "like a balloon" (178).

Part 2, Chapters 1-11 Analysis

The book's main themes of innovation, discovery, and exploration are emphasized in these chapters. Professor Aronnax tells Captain Nemo his ship is a century ahead of its time, regretting that "the secret of such an invention should die with its inventor!" (135). As befits the speculative fiction genre, Verne imagines the possibilities of life in a self-sustainable submarine. One such innovation is Nemo's source of wealth—the scavenging of treasure from many shipwrecks, and an underwater coal mine for energy. Another is a geographical guess—the idea that there is an underwater passageway between the Black Sea and the Mediterranean Verne calls the Arabian tunnel. Unlike the recovery of shipwrecks, however, this is a physical impossibility—these two seas have dramatically different sea levels, which would be identical were they actually connected. Verne also predicts that underwater exploration could answer questions from Christian and pagan mythologies. Captain Nemo takes Professor Aronnax on an underwater excursion to the ancient ruins of Atlantis, confirming that this legendary city is real in Verne's universe. Verne hedges, however, when fact-checking the Bible—he is unwilling to have Nemo find evidence of Moses parting the Red Sea or to suggest such evidence doesn't exist.

Professor Aronnax is increasingly impressed by everything Captain Nemo shows him, eager to learn and study from a man he considers a "genie of the sea" (165). He comes to admire Captain Nemo's "stature" and "unshaken confidence" (165). When Captain Nemo saves the pearl diver, Professor Aronnax deems him to be courageous as well as empathetic. Although Ned wants to escape, Professor Aronnax starts displaying symptoms of what would later be termed Stockholm syndrome—the psychological condition of siding with one's captors.

Like the patrons of the explorers he valorizes, Nemo bestrides the underwater world like its owner. He takes credit for improving the designs of many technological inventions and the discovery of geological and geographical features. He also speaks of many of the places the *Nautilus* visits as belonging to him. Though Nemo has rejected European civilization, his submarine world is a microcosm of a colonial power, with him as an authoritarian ruler who colonizes other domains and claims them in his own name. Ironically, Captain Nemo tells Professor Aronnax he is, to his "last breath, one of them!", that is, people born in "an oppressed country" (131)—he comes from a place on the receiving end of the kind of treatment Nemo clearly disdains when practiced by another other than himself. When Captain Nemo shows Professor Aronnax the priceless treasure on the shipwreck in Vigo Bay, he defends his use of the riches by proclaiming that he is not "ignorant that there are suffering beings and oppressed races on the earth, miserable creatures to console, victims to avenge" (162), a revelation that explains some of Nemo's obsessions and behavior.

Part 2, Chapters 12-23

Part 2, Chapter 12 Summary: "Cachalots and Whales"

The *Nautilus* continues south, and Professor Aronnax wonders if they are heading to the pole. Ned has become almost silent with rage, his prolonged imprisonment clearly weighing on him. He hasn't studied as Professor Aronnax has and doesn't appreciate the sea. Professor Aronnax realizes the monotony must be "intolerable" (180) to Ned. But on that day, an event occurs that further agitates Ned. Sitting out on the platform, Ned spots a whale. He has never hunted whales in these seas, so Professor Aronnax suggests he ask Captain Nemo to chase them.

Captain Nemo does not support killing whales for sport. Captain Nemo then points to the cachalots, or sperm whales, eight miles away, calling them "terrible animals" (182). Ned asks to hunt them instead, but Captain Nemo decides to just use the *Nautilus* to disperse them using a steel spur. They watch as the cachalots head toward the whales, preparing to attack. Captain Nemo steers the ship, which acts as an enormous harpoon, tearing the cachalots apart "with its terrible spur" (184). The massacre continues for an hour until the remaining cachalots depart.

Once the *Nautilus* goes back to the surface, there are bodies floating all around the ship. Ned considers what the *Nautilus* just did to be "butchery" (184), not hunting. After that day, Ned becomes even more hostile toward Captain Nemo.

Part 2, Chapter 13 Summary: "The Iceberg"

As the *Nautilus* heads south, they encounter floating ice. Although the path ahead is crowded with ice packs, the ship is able to easily slip through. They sit on the platform in fur to protect themselves from the frigid air. There are currently three or four hours of night, but soon there will be "six months of darkness" (186).

On March 16, they enter the Antarctic Circle. They are surrounded by ice, but the ship moves seamlessly. Professor Aronnax marvels at the beauty of the ice, which Captain Nemo penetrates like a "battering ram" (186). The wind and fog make it impossible to see. On March 18, an iceberg totally blocks the path and they are surrounded by in impenetrable field of ice on all sides. They can go neither backward nor forward. Captain Nemo, however, insists to Professor Aronnax that they are not stuck, and can go even further south, all the way to the pole. As no man had ever tread there before, including Captain Nemo, Professor Aronnax wonders if it is a "mad enterprise" that only a "maniac would have conceived" (188). Nemo plans to pass underneath the iceberg, speculating that the ice does not go lower than 900 feet below the surface.

Captain Nemo's only reservation is that they may not be able to resurface. At some point they will need air, even if they fill the reservoirs to capacity. Professor Aronnax wonders if they can use the spur diagonally against the ice. Captain Nemo prepares the ship, filling the reservoirs, and it dives.

The ship finds the bottom of the iceberg, which is over a thousand feet deep. The *Nautilus* attempts to penetrate the iceberg to reach the surface, but to no avail. They should have surfaced four hours ago to replenish the air supply, but they can only ascend slowly on a diagonal. Finally, on March 19, Captain Nemo enters the saloon to announce they are in water.

Part 2, Chapter 14 Summary: "The South Pole"

Captain Nemo and two of his men, along with Professor Aronnax and Conseil take the small boat toward a stretch of land a few miles away, which is "perhaps a continent" (192). When they reach it, Professor Aronnax insists Captain Nemo be the first to step out onto the uncharted land. Professor Aronnax follows with Conseil, noting the soil is clearly of "volcanic origin" (192). While there is only slight vegetation, as well as some mollusks, mussels, and zoophytes, there are thousands of birds, including albatrosses, chionis, petrels, damiers, and penguins. Captain Nemo has his men hunt some of them. However, the sun does not appear, which makes it impossible to determine if they are at the pole.

On March 20, they return to land to use the sun to determine their location. They observe a large variety of seals and sea elephants, which measure 10 and a half yards in length. At noon, the sun is still not visible. They have one more day to get a reading before the sun disappears for six months. The next day, Professor Aronnax asks Ned to come with them, but is relieved when he refuses, as the seals would be too much temptation for him.

Aronnax heads out in the small boat with Captain Nemo, two men, and the instruments, including a chronometer, telescope, and barometer. They arrive on land and climb to the top of a peak. After two hours, they reach the summit, looking out over a vast stretch of rocks and ice to the south and east. The sun begins to head toward the horizon, and at noon, it disappears, which means they are at the pole. Captain Nemo takes possession of it in his own name. He unfurls a banner with an "N" embroidered on it in gold.

Part 2, Chapter 15 Summary: "Accident or Incident?"

On March 22, they depart the South Pole. The *Nautilus* descents 1,000 feet and heads north at 15 miles per hour. In the middle of the night, Professor Aronnax is thrown into the middle of the room by a "violent shock" (199). He heads into the saloon and finds the furniture flung everywhere. Ned speculates the ship has struck something and is now lying on its side. Professor Aronnax reads the manometer and determines they are still beneath the water's surface.

Professor Aronnax asks Nemo if there's been an incident, to which Captain Nemo replies there's actually been an accident. He reassures them the danger is not immediate, but the *Nautilus* is stranded: An enormous iceberg has turned over and struck the ship. When the base of an iceberg heats up, it changes the center of gravity, potentially causing it to flip. This one has glided under the ship's hull and raised it, causing the ship to turn on its side. They are trying to empty the reservoirs to help the ship return to equilibrium. The ship is rising, but so is the block of ice. Professor Aronnax worries they will eventually hit the top part of the iceberg, causing the ship to get crushed.

After 10 minutes, the ship manages to right itself. They are in open water but surrounded by walls of ice on both sides, as well as above and below. The saloon gleams with intense light from the ice, shining in every color. It looks like a "dazzling mine of gems, particularly sapphires, their blue rays crossing with the green of emerald" (201-2). Even Ned remarks on the beauty of the scene, although he wonders if God intended man to see it. The ship heads backward to find a way out of the ice tunnel, but strikes ice going. They are trapped in the ice with no way out.

Part 2, Chapter 16 Summary: "Want of Air"

The *Nautilus* is surrounded by ice on all sides. There are two ways of dying in this situation: being crushed, or suffocating. The air reservoirs will be completely depleted in 48 hours, during which time they will attempt to escape. Professor Aronnax exclaims that he is relying on the courage of Ned and Conseil, while Ned proclaims he is "ready to do anything for the general safety" (204). They head out onto the bank of ice with Captain Nemo and the crew to dig a trench near the ship's port quarter. However, after 12 hours of work, they estimate it will take another five nights to finish the job. They only have enough air for two more days. Everyone is still determined to do what they can to survive.

The next morning, the side walls of ice are closing in on the ship. The only solution is to work faster than the walls are solidifying. On March 26, Professor Aronnax almost gives up when he realizes that the walls of the iceberg are continuing to grow thicker. Captain Nemo suddenly comes up with the idea of using jets of boiling water "injected by the pumps" (207) to raise the temperature. They implement the plan, but the process only raises the temperature by a few degrees.

On March 27, they still need to clear four yards of ice away, which it will take 48 hours. In that time, the air on the ship will run out. Professor Aronnax begins to experience the effects of running out of oxygen: He is dizzy and his head aches. With one yard to go, Captain Nemo decides to crush the remaining ice with the ship and head out into open water. The ship descends, and then heads north under the iceberg. Professor Aronnax is in agony, turning purple from lack of oxygen. Suddenly he is able to breathe—Ned and Conseil are using the last of the oxygen from the diving apparatus to supply him with air. They are 20 feet from the surface under a sheet of ice. The ship crashes through like a "battering-ram" (210) and reaches the surface. Air rushes in.

Part 2, Chapter 17 Summary: "From Cape Horn to the Amazon"

Professor Aronnax finds himself on the platform, unsure of how he got there. He, Ned, and Conseil breathe in the air without restraint. Professor Aronnax thanks his two companions for saving his life. Ned proclaims that when he finally leaves the "infernal *Nautilus*" (211), Professor Aronnax will come with him. However, Professor Aronnax worries Nemo will take them to the "deserted seas" (211) of the Pacific, where their journey began. They have forgotten the ordeal in the South Pole and think only of the future.

On April 1, they see the mountains of Terra del Fuego to the west, followed by the Falkland Islands. Professor Aronnax observes fish unique to the sea around the Falklands. The *Nautilus* follows the coast of South America heading north, traveling quickly past the populated coast of Brazil, to the dismay of Ned. They descend on April 9 to the "lowest depth of the submarine valley" (213) between Sierra Leone in Africa and Cape Ran Roque in South America and rise suddenly again on April 11 as they cross the equator. Although the Guianas are only 20 miles west, the waves are too rough to make an escape attempt.

Professor Aronnax continues his studies as the ship stays on the surface. The nets bring in zoophytes, fish, and reptiles. Of particular note are the 15-inch-long eels with "pointed snouts" (214) that travel along the current of the Amazon, yard-long little sharks with many rows of teeth, and 20-ounce ray that "formed a perfect disc" (214). On April 12, they sail near the Dutch coast and observe "peaceable and inoffensive" manatees (215) animals that serve an essential function by destroying weeds that are an obstruction to tropical rivers. Aronnax explains that since the manatees have been hunted to near extinction, the unchecked growth of weeds have "poisoned the air" (215), causing diseases like yellow fever. Nevertheless, the ship's crew kills half a dozen of them to eat, as well as many other fish and fresh turtles with "exquisite flavour" (216). After a successful day of fishing, the ship departs the shores of the Amazon.

Part 2, Chapter 18 Summary: "The Poulps"

Professor Aronnax, Ned, and Conseil converse at length about their possible escape. They have been on the *Nautilus* for six months and traveled 17,000 leagues. Captain Nemo has recently become "grave, more retired, less sociable" (216)—he will not let them go of his own volition. Professor Aronnax feels shunned by the Captain, who rarely makes an appearance.

Near the Bahamas, Professor Aronnax explains to Ned that they might expect to see enormous poulps, or giant squid. There are legends dating back to ancient times of poulps taking down whole ships with mouths "like gulfs" (218). The most compelling modern evidence comes from the real-life Captain Bouguer and the crew of the *Alector,* who saw a "monstrous cuttle-fish swimming in the water" (219) in 1861. "Bouguer's cuttle-fish" (219) measured six yards, had eight tentacles, three hearts, and eyes in the back of its head.

Ned runs to the window, claiming to see Bouguer's cuttlefish. Professor and Conseil look outside and observe "an immense cuttle-fish, being eight yards long" (219) swimming quickly toward the ship. It has eight arms, a mouth like a beak, long rows of sharp teeth, and weighs thousands of pounds. Professor Aronnax counts seven others like the first. The *Nautilus* rises to the surface but stops moving. Captain Nemo and his lieutenant decide to fight the poulps "man to beast" (220)—one of them is caught in the ship's blades, which is why they have stopped moving. He plans to kill them all with hatchets, and Ned offers to help with his harpoon.

As they remove the panel to go outside, tentacles slip into the opening. Two of them grab one of the crew members. He cries for help in French, which stirs emotions in Professor Aronnax as he fears for his fellow countryman. As a dozen creatures encroach on the ship, everyone attacks with their weapons. The creature holding the crewmember sprays a black liquid that blinds them all and disappears. One of the creatures knocks Ned to the ground with its tentacles and prepares to eat him. Suddenly, Captain Nemo plunges his ax into the creature's jaws, and Ned stabs his harpoon into its triple heart. The creatures, "vanquished and mutilated" (222), head back into the sea.

Part 2, Chapter 19 Summary: "The Gulf Stream"

Captain Nemo is devastated at the loss of another companion. The fact that the man had spoken his native French at the end, instead of the language used on board the ship, deeply moves Professor Aronnax. Captain Nemo shuts himself inside his room, "sad and irresolute" (223). The ship stays in the same place for 10 days before finally resuming its journey north following the Gulf Stream.

The ship seems to be sailing at random, which gives them some possibility for escape. There are ships around and they are not more than 30 miles from the American coast. However, the weather is not favorable and there are lots of storms. Still, soon they will be near Ned's native Quebec. Professor Aronnax has also begun to feel homesick after seven months on the *Nautilus*. Ned suggests he talk to Captain Nemo that night.

Professor Aronnax finds Captain Nemo, who impatiently asks him what he wants. Nemo is working on a manuscript in many different languages of his studies of the sea. He wishes it to be put into a case for the last survivor on the ship to throw into the water. Professor Aronnax offers to keep it for Nemo if he will free them, but Captain Nemo's feelings about letting them go remain the same. Aronnax bristles at Nemo's desire to "impose actual slavery" (226) on them, but Captain Nemo insists he doesn't keep him on board "for my pleasure" (226).

Professor Aronnax relates his conversation to Ned and Conseil. Ned says they should escape regardless of the weather when they are near Long Island. However, a hurricane descends upon them on May 13. The ship gets tossed around by gigantic waves. A cyclone approaches. Lightening crackles all around. Captain Nemo stands out on the platform "courting a death worthy of himself, a death by lightning" (228). Finally, the ship descends and the water becomes so calm that one would hardly know a hurricane raged above.

Part 2, Chapter 20 Summary: "From Latitude 47º 24' to Longitude 17º 28'"

The storm forces them to sail northeast, so there is no chance of escaping to the American coast. Ned isolates himself "in despair" (228), but Conseil and Professor Aronnax stay together. The ship dives to avoid the dense fog that has shipwrecked so many others. On May 15, they are south of the Bank of Newfoundland, where there are blocks of ice and "large heaps of organic matter" (229). On May 17, Professor Aronnax spots an underwater electric cable for telegraph communication on the sea floor—the remains of a failed attempt in 1863 to run a cable measuring 2,000 miles. A better cable was eventually constructed and was successfully run under the Atlantic.

On May 28, they are 120 miles from Ireland but begin to head south. Professor Aronnax is unsure where they are going. Captain Nemo seems "gloomier than ever" (231). The ship travels in circles and appears to be trying to find a particular location. On June 1, Captain Nemo takes the sun's altitude and cryptically pronounces, "It is here" (231). The ship descends into the water.

Professor Aronnax sees a "large protuberance" (231)—the sunken ship *Marseillais.* After it participated in several battles. In 1794, its name was changed to "The *Avenger*" (232) and it was tasked with escorting corn from America under Admiral Van Stable. It encountered an English vessel and preferred to sink with all 356 crew on board rather than surrender. When Aronnax identifies it, Captain Nemo declares the renamed vessel to have "A good name!" (232).

Part 2, Chapter 21 Summary: "A Hecatomb"

Professor Aronnax realizes Captain Nemo is a man with a "hatred" that "could never weaken" (232). As the *Nautilus* rises again to the surface, they hear a loud sound in the air—the sound of a gunshot coming from a "man-of-war" (233) that is now six miles away from the *Nautilus*. Ned says if the ship comes within a mile of them, he's going to throw himself into the water and advises Professor Aronnax and Conseil to do the same. Whether the ship is Russian, American, French, or English, it will take them on board.

Something heavy lands in the water nearby and they realize the vessel is firing on the *Nautilus*. Professor Aronnax wonders if everyone figured out that the monster cetacean was actually a submarine vessel and are now out to destroy it. Maybe Captain Nemo had attacked some other ship in an act of vengeance when Professor Aronnax, Ned, and Conseil were drugged that one night. Perhaps nations had banded together to destroy "a man who had vowed a deadly hatred against them" (234). If this is the case, the ship attacking them would view any man on board the *Nautilus* as an enemy, ruining their escape plan.

Ned signals to the other ship, but as he waves his handkerchief in the air, Captain Nemo strikes him down and angrily asks if Ned wishes "to be pierced by the spur of the *Nautilus* before it is hurled at this vessel?" (234). As a shot strikes the *Nautilus*, Nemo commands Professor Aronnax, Ned, and Conseil to go inside because he plans to sink the other vessel. Captain Nemo refuses to identify the other ship, but tells Professor Aronnax that because of a man on that ship, he lost everything —"country, wife, children, father, and mother" (235).

Professor Aronnax, Ned, and Conseil agree they would rather sink with the other ship than be part of Captain Nemo's revenge. However, the *Nautilus* descends and they are once again trapped. The *Nautilus* speeds up and attacks the other vessel with its spur. Professor Aronnax screams and hears "rattlings and scrapings" (238), feeling like he's losing his mind. Captain Nemo watches the other ship sink: Men are "clinging to the masks, struggling under the water" (238). Aronnax looks at Captain Nemo, now a "perfect archangel of hatred" (238) watching the ship go down unblinkingly. Captain Nemo then turns to a portrait of a young woman and two children and bursts out crying.

Part 2, Chapter 22 Summary: "The Last Words of Captain Nemo"

Professor Aronnax feels "an insurmountable horror" (239) of Captain Nemo and deems his vengeance too extreme. He has terrible nightmares and keeps seeing the vessel sinking. He feels as though all time has stopped and refuses to see Captain Nemo or any of the crew for several days. Conseil watches him to make sure he doesn't kill himself.

One morning, Ned wakes Professor Aronnax from a "painful and unhealthy" (239) sleep and tells him they're leaving tomorrow night. Everyone on the *Nautilus* appears "stupefied" (240) and unidentifiable land appears to be about 20 miles away. The wind and water are rough, but Ned has put provisions in the small boat and is ready to "fly" (240). If anyone catches him, he's prepared to die, to which Professor Aronnax adds they "will die together" (240).

Professor Aronnax goes to the saloon, ultimately deciding he doesn't want to see Captain Nemo. He looks one last time at the priceless masterpieces of art and the "wonders of nature" (240), trying to retain an image of them in his mind. He then goes back to his room to get ready. He is agitated and anxious. He rehashes every event that has transpired on the *Nautilus* since he came aboard. The image of Captain Nemo grows to "superhuman proportions" (241) in his mind, becoming "a man of the waters, the genie of the sea" (241).

Waiting for the escape attempt to start, Aronnax hears the organ playing "a sad harmony to an undefinable chant" (241). He listens with every fiber of his being, and finds himself in the same "musical ecstasy" (241) as Captain Nemo, "which was drawing him in spirit to the end of life" (241). He suddenly realizes he has to walk through the saloon and worries that a single look or gesture from Captain Nemo will keep him from leaving. As Aronnax silently moves through the room, Captain Nemo sighs and stands up, seeming to glide "like a spectre" (242). He is crying, "Almighty God! Enough! Enough!" (242). Professor Aronnax hurries to the boat. Ned starts to loosen the bolts that connect the boat to the *Nautilus* when they hear the crew repeating "The maelstrom!" (242) over and over. They are near Norway where the waters form a violent whirlpool called "the 'Navel of the Ocean'" (242). Nothing can escape it—whales, ships, and white bears have all been sacrificed to it. They are slowly being sucked in and can hear the sounds of water breaking on the rocks below. The bolts holding the boat to the *Nautilus* suddenly tear away and the men are flung "like a stone from a sling" (243). Professor Aronnax hits his head and loses consciousness.

Part 2, Chapter 23 Summary: "Conclusion"

Professor Aronnax does not know how he, Ned, and Conseil escaped the whirlpool, but when he regains consciousness, he is in a fisherman's hut on the Loffoden Isles with Ned and Conseil holding his hands. They all embrace. Professor Aronnax's records of their journey are intact, and he maintains that every detail is accurate. He doesn't know if he'll be believed, but he has "a right to speak of the seas" (244), having crossed 20,000 leagues in less than 10 months.

The fate of Captain Nemo and the *Nautilus* is unknown. Professor Aronnax doesn't know if Captain Nemo's manuscript will survive, or if his nationality or name will ever be revealed. He hopes that the *Nautilus* made it through the maelstrom and wishes that Captain Nemo's journey's through the sea will conquer his hatred—that the "philosopher" will replace the "judge" (244) and that his destiny will be "sublime" (244). Only two men can answer the question posed 3,000 years ago by Ecclesiastes: "That which is far off and exceeding deep, who can find it out" (244). Those two men are Captain Nemo and Professor Aronnax.

Part 2, Chapters 12-23 Analysis

Captain Nemo's character changes dramatically in this section, and Professor Aronnax and the reader finally learn the purpose of his travels around the sea. The first indication that he is yielding to his baser instincts is his reckless slaughter of the cachalots with the spur of the *Nautilus*. Ned accuses Captain Nemo of butchery, and Captain Nemo proudly admits to "a massacre" (184). As Captain Nemo allows his need for control and revenge to take over, his turn toward a darker emotional state is reflected in the ship's encounters with more harrowing natural enemies. They battle giant, terrifying poulps, "a freak of nature" (220) that weigh thousands of pounds and have bird beaks for mouths. At the South Pole, the ship gets stuck in ice, and they all nearly suffocate. Professor Aronnax ultimately comes to see the man he once admired as a destroyer of worlds, a "perfect archangel of hatred" (238). When Captain Nemo sinks the ship holding the man responsible for destroying Nemo's family, Professor Aronnax watches in horror as Nemo's thirst for revenge wreaks violent vengeance, dooming to death the man-o-war's entire crew for the actions of one person. Regardless of the losses Captain Nemo has suffered, Professor Aronnax decides that he has no justification for sinking the ship.

As Professor Aronnax finds Captain Nemo increasingly more horrifying, his bond with Ned and Conseil grows stronger. His "two brave friends" (210) sacrifice the air for themselves to save Professor Aronnax, giving him "life drop by drop" (210). When Ned pushes more aggressively for his freedom, Professor Aronnax finally throws his full support behind him. He agrees with Ned that "this must come to an end" (224), confronting Nemo about their endless captivity.

Ultimately, Captain Nemo's reckless behavior sends his ship hurtling toward the whirlpool, and Professor Aronnax to his freedom—along with Ned and Conseil. The "irresistible violence" (243) of the maelstrom is a stark reflection of Captain Nemo's desire for revenge. Although Captain Nemo's fate is unknown, Professor Aronnax sincerely hopes that the innovator, philosopher, and explorer he found so intriguing, and greatly admired, has eclipsed the man possessed by "the spirit of vengeance" (244). The book ends with the final message that the destructive power of technology can undermine its potential for innovation, exploration, and discovery.

Character Analysis

Professor Pierre Aronnax

Professor Aronnax is the main character and narrator of the book. He is a 40-year-old Frenchman who works as an Assistant Professor at the Museum of Natural History in Paris. He previously published a two-volume work called *Mysteries of the Great Submarine Grounds*, which Captain Nemo has a copy of on board the *Nautilus.* Aronnax has an adventurous spirit, and travels to various locations to study natural history with his servant Conseil and a menagerie that includes a wild pig. He passes his time on the *Nautilus* studying marine life, and finds the work fulfilling until Captain Nemo's rage compromises Professor Aronnax's morals. Up to that point, Aronnax feels admiration and respect for Captain Nemo, judging him to be capable, intelligent, and of "unparalleled courage" (131). Professor Aronnax maintains a loyal friendship with Conseil and Ned Land—his two companions on the *Nautilus*—which helps them to survive their escape from the ship.

Conseil

Conseil is Professor Aronnax's loyal servant who will do anything for his master, including putting Professor Aronnax's life above his own. He is a 30-year-old "Flemish boy" (9), who for 10 years has accompanied Professor Aronnax on his journeys, helping him with his research. Professor Aronnax describes Conseil as "quick with his hands" (10), in excellent health, and always obliging. His only fault, according to Professor Aronnax, is that he is "ceremonious to a degree" (10) and will only ever address Professor Aronnax as "master." Aboard the *Nautilus*, Conseil helps to save Professor Aronnax's life more than once, building a lasting friendship between the two men.

Ned Land

Ned Land is a Canadian harpooner who knows "no equal in his dangerous occupation" (13). He is 40 years old with a tall stature, strong build, and passionate temperament, especially when challenged. He is reserved and serious, but attracts attention with his "boldness of look" (14). Ned forms an immediate friendship with Professor Aronnax on board the *Abraham*

Lincoln that grows stronger during their captivity on the *Nautilus*, even though Ned has little interest in marine fauna besides his ever-present passion for hunting. Ned's desire for personal liberty is more pronounced than that of Professor Aronnax or Conseil, and he is the most aggressive about planning their escape from the *Nautilus*, often declaring that he is ready to die rather than remain imprisoned. Ned's last name is a strong indicator of his yearning to escape underwater life.

Captain Nemo

Captain Nemo is the commander of the *Nautilus*. He is self-confident, energetic, and courageous, while also possessing a calm demeanor that masks a "highly nervous temperament" (33). His age is unclear and could range, according to Professor Aronnax, from 35 to 50. He is tall with a "straight nose" and "beautiful teeth" (33). His eyes are set widely apart, which allows his range of vision across the horizon to be particularly acute. Captain Nemo's character is mysterious, along with his past. His rejection of humanity has driven him to an isolated life at sea, almost completely devoid of human contact save for his crew, Professor Aronnax, Ned, and Conseil. Despite his cynicism toward humankind, he is generous toward the oppressed peoples of the world, and passionate about scientific knowledge, innovation, and discovery. The *Nautilus* is the most technologically advanced ship in the world, which Captain Nemo uses to push the boundaries of what's possible, often despite the moral implications. His desire for knowledge is gradually eclipsed over the course of the book by his desire for revenge for the destruction of his family.

Commander Farragut

Commander Farragut is the captain of the *Abraham Lincoln*. He is, according to Professor Aronnax, the "soul" (12) of his ship. He holds an unshakeable opinion that the mysterious object in the water is a cetacean. His absolute goal is to "rid the seas of it" (12), which motivates him to continue searching, even as chances of success grow slimmer. As Professor Aronnax summarizes of Captain Farragut, either he "would kill the narwhal, or the narwhal would kill" him (12).

Themes

Nature versus Technology

The book emphasizes the wonders of the natural world and the advanced technology Captain Nemo creates. Both are fascinating and dangerous, sometimes coexisting seamlessly, and other times set against one another, especially as Captain Nemo pushes the boundaries of exploration and turns toward revenge. Although the *Nautilus* is often successful in escaping harrowing situations, its fate is ultimately unknown as it gets sucked in toward the maelstrom.

The *Nautilus* is a technological marvel. It is capable of great speeds and depths, has many tools aboard that are perfected versions of previous inventions, and, as Captain Nemo brags to Professor Aronnax, has "No defects to be afraid of" (55). Professor Aronnax deems the ship "at least a century before its time, perhaps an era" (135). With its advanced capabilities, the ship seems perfectly designed for its intended surroundings. The *Nautilus* looks like a sea creature— initially mistaken for a narwhal, it blends into the marine environment. Fish and other marine life swim along with it and provide entertainment, and it enables scholars like Professor Aronnax to survey and explore the otherwise inaccessible ocean floor. The water also provides essential resources for the ship, including food and fuel. The sea "supplies all my wants," explains Captain Nemo (43).

The natural world is equally as wondrous, filled with mystery and beauty. Professor Aronnax, Captain Nemo, and Conseil study many amazing kinds of sea plants and creatures. "What a spectacle!" proclaims Professor Aronnax when the panels in the saloon open for the first time and he views the marine life from within the water's depths—an "enchanting vision" that passes before his "dazzled eyes" (60).

However, as Captain Nemo pushes the limits of discovery and begins to seek vengeance, the *Nautilus* increasingly goes up against nature. As the *Nautilus* becomes more destructive, so does the marine environment. The ship and its crew battle a number of natural foes, including sharks, giant poulps, violent storms, and the Antarctic ice. One of the poulps kills a crewmember; when the ship is trapped in ice, the crew is under threat of suffocation, starvation, or being crushed to death, and Professor Aronnax feels as though he is "going to die" (220). When they encounter the maelstrom, their "horror was at its height" at the "whirlpool from which no vessel ever escapes" (243). The power of the natural environment becomes the ultimate force to be reckoned with, and it is unknown if Captain Nemo and the *Nautilus* survive it.

Liberty versus Imprisonment

A major theme throughout the book is the contrast between liberty and imprisonment. Professor Aronnax, Ned, and Conseil are held hostage on board the *Nautilus*. Captain Nemo makes the terms of their situation on the *Nautilus* clear—they must stay on board to keep the existence of the ship a secret.

Although they often enjoy their experiences, particularly Professor Aronnax, they never mistake their luxurious captivity for freedom. When Captain Nemo proclaims that Professor Aronnax, Ned, and Conseil can do whatever they want aboard the ship, Professor Aronnax responds that "this liberty is only what every prisoner has of pacing his prison," adding that it "cannot suffice" (41). Professor Aronnax, even when he still personally admires Nemo and marvels at his newfound access to undersea nature, insists to Captain Nemo that holding them captive is "cruelty" (41) and laments that their "only course was to submit" (176). Professor Aronnax eventually tells Captain Nemo that their imprisonment echoes "actual slavery" (226), and every slave has a right to gain their freedom.

Ned is the most adamant about escaping. He finds his circumstances "intolerable," as he is accustomed "to a life of liberty and activity" (180). He tells Professor Aronnax and Conseil he is waiting for a "favourable opportunity" to leave the *Nautilus* (146)—and makes it clear that he would be happy to die in the attempt. Professor Aronnax and Conseil agree, now willing to risk their lives for their freedom. "Liberty," insists Ned when he is prepared to face a tumultuous sea to escape, "is worth paying for" (157).

Innovation, Exploration, and Discovery

The novel presents innovation, exploration, and discovery as ways of countering hatred and anger. Professor Aronnax constantly desires to learn and study, and for much of the book finds Captain Nemo an invaluable guide, even referring to him as a "genie of the sea" (165, 241).

Innovation drives the first part of the novel. Captain Nemo impresses Professor Aronnax with the unbelievably high-tech submarine he pilots. He shows off inventions like his electricity-powered navigational system, a diving apparatus that allows them to walk on the bottom of the sea, and other technological novelties. Nemo's ingenuity is one of the reasons Professor Aronnax is drawn to him, and deems him a man he understands. After a tour of the ship, Professor Aronnax exclaims that it is "a marvelous boat" (55) and that Captain Nemo is "an engineer of a very high order" (51).

The *Nautilus* is an exploration vessel, traveling to remote regions and depths that no one has ever been before. Their initial voyages are scientifically minded: Professor Aronnax is "dazzled" (60) by the wide range of aquatic life he observes and analyzes, and which are often named and described in detail. Of their first submarine excursion into the forest to hunt, Professor Aronnax states that "Words are impotent to relate such wonders!" (68). Besides zoology and botany, Professor Aronnax gets a taste of anthropology when Captain Nemo takes him pearl diving, and later reveals an underwater cemetery in a coral reef.

The novel is also fascinated with the idea of discovery. For verisimilitude, Verne often alludes to the expeditions of famed French explorers, including Lapérouse and Dumont d'Urville. Their real-life voyages buttress the novel's invented ones, as when Captain Nemo shows Professor Aronnax the lost civilization of Atlantis, discovers a tunnel between the Black Sea and the Mediterranean, and becomes the first person to land at the South Pole. The novel draws on firsthand accounts of explorers when Professor Aronnax declares he can hardly believe he is "touching with my hand those ruins a thousand generations old," and "walking on the very spot where the contemporaries of the first man had walked" (168). Although Captain Nemo's character takes a dark turn, Professor Aronnax hopes his hatred is extinguished by his continued "peaceful exploration of the sea!" (244).

Friendship

The survival of Professor Aronnax, Ned, and Conseil, both on the *Nautilus* and during their escape, relies on their deep-seated friendship. Professor Aronnax is always dedicated to the needs of his two companions, even when he is still impressed with Captain Nemo. His dedication grows even stronger as Captain Nemo becomes increasingly obsessed with revenge.

Aronnax supports Ned's desire to escape, and never wavers in his allegiance to Ned and Conseil—who demonstrate that they are willing to sacrifice their own lives to save Professor Aronnax when they give him the last of the oxygen in Antarctica. He refers to them as his "two brave friends" (210) and feels he will never be able to repay Ned and Conseil for "such devotion" (211). They are finally able to escape together, embracing "each other heartily" (243). Their survival would not have been possible without their loyalty to one another.

The Perils of Vengeance

The book points out the pitfalls of being motivated by vengeance, which undermines positive aspirations and ideals. Despite Captain Nemo's solidarity with the oppressed, he cannot overcome his need to take revenge on those who have wronged him. As he begins to use the ship as a weapon of destruction, rather than as a tool for exploration, his competence unravels. Captain Nemo's need for revenge becomes his ultimate undoing, pushing the besotted Professor Aronnax away and sending the *Nautilus* into the whirlpool.

Over the course of the book, Nemo grows isolated, exhibiting "altered spirits" and "taciturnity" (225) which cause Professor Aronnax to "view things in a different light" (225). Captain Nemo also becomes more aggressive, as his violent slaughter of the cachalots attests. However, it is his desire for revenge that becomes his dominating quality. After they succeed in fending off the large poulps, Captain Nemo tells Ned that he "owed myself this revenge!" (222). When he insists on destroying the ship that attacks them just to get at one man, Professor Aronnax describes Nemo as "terrible to hear" and "still more terrible to see" (234). Regardless of the actions of the other boat, Captain Nemo "had no right to punish thus" (239). Captain Nemo become unrecognizable in his anger, a "terrible avenger, a perfect archangel of hatred" (238).

Despite his intelligence and passion for discovery, Captain Nemo is unable to conquer his inner rage. His penchant for destruction is reflected in the violence of the maelstrom, which sucks in any ship that comes near it, crushing it into the rocks below. As Captain Nemo can't escape his hatred, he also can't escape the whirlpool. The *Nautilus* heads directly into it as Captain Nemo plays "a sad harmony" (241) on his organ. Although Captain Nemo's fate is unknown, Professor Aronnax hopes he has survived and that "the contemplation of so many wonders extinguish for ever the spirit of vengeance!" (244).

Symbols & Motifs

The Sea

The entire book takes place in the sea, which represents the power of nature. As Captain Nemo proclaims, "The sea is everything" (43). Despite Nemo's technological advancements and his increasing ability to manipulate his environment, best embodied in the existence of the *Nautilus*, he and his crew are still forced to reckon with the uncompromising environment of the sea. While the sea offers "wonderful sights" (78) and sustains abundant life—often described in great detail by Professor Aronnax—it also has the power to take life away, as evidenced by the shipwrecks the *Nautilus* encounters and the lost underwater civilization of Atlantis. The crew of the *Nautilus* also faces tremendous dangers from weather, ocean conditions, and sea predators: giant poulps, sharks, strong storms, Antarctic ice, and the giant maelstrom at the end of the book, which leaves Captain Nemo's fate unknown. While the *Nautilus* is a powerful ship, the sea, with its "awful mysteries" (78), often presents itself as its direct foe, demonstrating that even the most sophisticated technologies in the world can be humbled by nature.

The Nautilus

The *Nautilus* represents the destructive potential of technological innovation when taken to its most extreme point. The ship is a marvel of engineering and is often used for exploration and learning. However, there is a dark underside to the benefits of a ship that can withstand the pressures of the ocean's depths. In the hands of an obsessive, sometimes overly self-confident captain, the *Nautilus* often pushes the limits of discovery, as when it heads under the Antarctic ice. Ned proclaims that, while the ice under the water is beautiful, he worries "we are seeing here things which God never intended man to see" (202), implying that Nemo's belief that the underwater world belongs to him is hubris that will be divinely punished.

But there are further problems to controlling such a powerful machine, as it also becomes the ultimate weapon. As Captain Nemo succumbs to his desire for vengeance, he turns the ship into the ultimate weapon of destruction. He slaughters several cachalots with the spur of his ship, covering the sea "with mutilated bodies" (184), an act Ned condemns as "butchery" (184). Soon after, Captain Nemo uses the *Nautilus* to destroy a ship he has been pursuing all along, one he believes carries a man responsible for the destruction of Nemo's family. Professor Aronnax, Ned, and Conseil all morally oppose this vicious act of revenge, which murders an entire ship's worth of crew to kill one man, even a guilty one.

Professor Aronnax once lauded Captain Nemo as courageous, admirable, and a man he understood. However, the man whom he previously viewed as a "genie of the sea" (165, 241) has become "a perfect archangel of hatred" (238). He feels "an insurmountable horror for Captain Nemo" (239), as the latter's "spirit of vengeance" (244) has eclipsed his quest for knowledge. The unrivaled power and capabilities of the *Nautilus* have allowed Captain Nemo to employ it as an instrument of terror, showing the dangers of technology when it falls into the hands of a "terrible avenger" (238).

Nemo's Insignia

Nemo's insignia, which consists of the letter "N," symbolizes Captain Nemo's ego and his desire for control—through his insignia, Nemo crafts an underwater empire he hopes to rule. The "N" is engraved on dinnerware and embroidered on the banners Nemo unfurls at the South Pole, staking his claim on the continent the way a country's explorer would with a flag, taking "possession of this part of the globe, equal to one-sixth of the known continents" (198).

Conversely, however, the fact that he has given up his real name and uses an enigmatic pseudonym that means "no name" undercuts his ability to truly assert ownership over the seas; his desire to stamp an "N" on everything points out that ultimately the person who claims to own the underwater world is literally no one—the implication of Nemo's chosen name.

The Pearl Diver

Captain Nemo risks his life to save the diver and rewards him with a bag of pearls—an incident that illustrates Captain Nemo's empathy and altruism, which exist despite his rejection of humanity and desire for vengeance. Captain Nemo identifies with the pearl diver, a member of an exploited population that Nemo claims as his origin. As Captain Nemo tells Professor Aronnax, he is not "ignorant that there are suffering beings and oppressed races on this earth" (162) and instead stands in solidarity with the world's "oppressed races" and "individuals" (162), driven by a sense of duty to those who are like himself—standing against an "oppressor" (235) who has destroyed everything he once loved.

Contextual Analysis

Authorial Context

Jules Verne was born in Nantes, France, in 1828 and began writing at an early age. He went to several different schools in Nantes before enrolling in law school in Paris in 1847 at the urging of his father, who wanted him to take up the family legal practice. While in law school, Verne continued writing and frequented the literary salons of Paris. Through his visits to the salons, he established contacts with authors, magazine editors, and stage directors, who encouraged and aided his career. Verne was heavily influenced by the writings of Victor Hugo, the author of *The Hunchback of Notre-Dame*, published in 1831.

When Verne graduated law school in 1851, he began publishing his stories and articles in magazines. He also wrote plays and musical comedies for the Théâtre Lyrique. Although his father offered him the family law practice in 1852, Verne declined, deciding instead to pursue his career as an author. He published his first novel, *Five Weeks in a Balloon*, in 1863.

Verne's works often combine adventure, travel, history, geography, and science, with an emphasis on recent innovations and discoveries. His most successful novels are *Journey to the Center of the Earth,* published in 1864, *Twenty Thousand Leagues Under the Sea,* published in 1869, and *Around the World in Eighty Days,* published in 1872. During his lifetime, Verne achieved great fame as an author and became rich from his works. He died in 1905 at the age of 77 in his home in Amiens after suffering from diabetes and a stroke.

Although Verne was considered a popular genre writer when he was alive, he gained a reputation posthumously as a serious literary author, particularly in France. His works became an influential part of the French literary canon, and gained a similar reputation in the English-speaking world. Verne is considered one of the founders of the science fiction genre, predicting several major technological developments in his works. Since 1979, he has remained the second most-translated author in the world.

Important Quotes

1. "For some time past, vessels had been met by 'an enormous thing,' a long object, spindle-shaped, occasionally phosphorescent, and infinitely larger and more rapid in its movements than a whale."
(Part 1, Chapter 1, Page 1)

The opening paragraphs of the book discuss a mysterious object in the water that many seafarers had been encountering in their travels. Until 1876, not much information was known about it. Those who saw it, however, agreed that it was huge and traveled through the water quickly. The strange object gripped the public imagination around the world and was considered an imminent danger to sea travelers.

2. "Three seconds after reading the letter of the honourable Secretary of marine, I felt that my true vocation, the sole end of my life, was to chase this disturbing monster, and purge it from the world."
(Part 1, Chapter 3, Page 9)

Professor Aronnax, the narrator of the story, receives a letter from the United States Government. Signed by the Secretary of Marine, it asks him to join an expedition on the Abraham Lincoln *in pursuit of the mysterious object in the water—which everyone, including Professor Aronnax, has determined to be a monster. While Professor Aronnax had given no thought to such an endeavor before he receives the letter, he decides—a few seconds after reading it—that it is now his sole purpose in life. He feels it is his calling to pursue the monster and rid the world of such a menacing threat.*

3. "The entire ship's crew was undergoing a nervous excitement, of which I can give no idea: they could not eat, they could not sleep—twenty times a day, a misconception or an optical illusion of some sailor seated on the taffrail, would cause dreadful perspirations, and those emotions, twenty times repeated, kept us in a state of excitement so violent that a reaction was unavoidable."
(Part 1, Chapter 5, Page 18)

Once onboard the Abraham Lincoln, *the whole crew is invested in finding the monster. Men of all ranks watch day and night, which keeps the mood tense. Although they often end up chasing a whale, everyone is constantly on edge with the prospect of finding the creature. Captain Farragut has also offers a prize of two thousand dollars to the first man who spots it, which adds to the constant energy and excitement.*

4. "There was no doubt about it! This monster, this natural phenomenon that had puzzled the learned world, and overthrown and misled the imagination of seamen of both hemisphere, was, it must be owned, a still more astonishing phenomenon, inasmuch as it was simply a human construction."
(Part 1, Chapter 7, Page 30)

*A collision between the monster and the*Abraham Lincoln *throws Professor Aronnax overboard and into the sea. Conseil follows and they struggle to save one another from drowning. Suddenly, as Professor Aronnax feels himself slipping into the sea, Ned Land pulls him and Conseil onto the monster. He quickly realizes that the monster is not a natural creature of the sea, but a man-made machine. He—along with the rest of the world—has been fooled into thinking it was some type of animal. He finds that this makes it even more impressive and interesting.*

5. "A flash of anger and disdain kindle in the eyes of the Unknown, and I had a glimpse of a terrible past in the life of this man. Not only had he put himself beyond the pale of human laws, but he had made himself independent of them, free in the strictest acceptation of the word, quite beyond their reach!"
(Part 1, Chapter 9, Page 40)

After Professor Aronnax, Ned Land, and Conseil board the ship, they are held in a cabin until Captain Nemo confronts them about chasing him around the ocean. Captain Nemo has deliberately removed himself from society and does not appreciate their intrusion. Professor Aronnax believes that Nemo has fled a tormented past, finding a new life in the water that frees him from the rules that govern society. His freedom is absolute and he does not have to answer to anyone but himself.

6. "These are the only ties that bind me to the earth. But I had done with the world on the day when my *Nautilus* plunged for the first time beneath the waters. That day I bought my last volumes, my last pamphlets, my last papers, and from that time I wish to think that men no longer think or write."
(Part 1, Chapter 10, Page 44)

Professor Aronnax, Ned, and Conseil become Captain Nemo's prisoners on the ship, but they are allowed to roam about freely. Professor Aronnax is impressed by the 12,000 volumes that line the shelves of his extensive library. Captain Nemo explains that his books are his only ties to society. In his mind, nothing else has been produced since the day he plunged into the ocean in the Nautilus. *The works are frozen in time—the only evidence of a past that no longer exists.*

7. "There sir! That is the perfection of vessels! And if it is true that the engineer has more confidence in the vessel than the builder, and the builder than the captain himself, you understand the trust I repose in my *Nautilus* for I am at once captain, builder, and engineer."
(Part 1, Chapter 12, Page 55)

Captain Nemo takes Professor Aronnax around the ship and explains how it works. He emphasizes that the design of the ship is flawless and built to perfection. It is not subject to the problems facing other ships that sail on the surface. He then states that he is the one who designed and constructed the ship, and therefore places his complete trust in it.

8. "'Ah!' thought I to myself, 'I understand the life of this man; he has made a world part for himself, in which he treasures all his greatest wonders.'"
(Part 1, Chapter 13, Page 60)

Professor Aronnax, Ned, and Conseil are in the saloon when the lights suddenly go out. Two iron panels open and reveal crystal windows that look out into the ocean, which is illuminated by light from the ship. The three men stare out in awe for two hours at all the aquatic life that passes before the windows. In those moments, professor Aronnax appreciates Captain Nemo's choice to live a life of isolation at sea. Captain Nemo resides in his own underwater world, where he can marvel at the treasures of the sea and have them all to himself.

9. "And now, how can I retrace the impression left upon me by that walk under the waters? Words are impotent to relate such wonders!"
(Part 1, Chapter 15, Page 68)

Captain Nemo, Professor Aronnax, and Conseil hunt in a submarine forest, suited up in heavy gear that makes it possible for them to walk on the ocean floor. With the sunlight shining through the water, they see a vast array of aquatic life. Professor Aronnax hardly has the words to describe the experience. Once again, Captain Nemo has shown him something that has rendered him in complete awe.

10. "What a scene! We were dumb; our hearts beat fast before this shipwreck, taken as it were from life, and photographed in its last moments."
(Part 1, Chapter 17, Page 79)

After traveling two thousand miles over the course of several days, Conseil spots a shipwreck through the window. They see five corpses—four men and a woman holding a baby. The steersman is still holding the wheel. They can only look out in silence at the ship's final moments. The tragic scene is a humbling moment and foreshadows several unfortunate events that will befall the Nautilus.

11. "Captain Nemo was before me, but I did not know him. His face was transfigured. His eyes flashed sullenly; his teeth were set; his stiff body, clenched fists, and head shrunk between his shoulders, betrayed the violent agitation that pervaded his whole frame."
(Part 1, Chapter 22, Page 107)

After the Nautilus *is freed from the rocks in the Torres Straits, it heads toward the Indian Ocean. As the ship loses sight of land, Professor Aronnax heads to the ship's platform. He finds Captain Nemo and his lieutenant having an agitated conversation and pointing to a spot on the horizon. When Professor Aronnax attempts to see what they are looking at through his telescope, Captain Nemo knocks it out of his hand. Professor Aronnax has only ever seen Captain Nemo be calm and barely recognizes him in his angered state. In that moment, Captain Nemo is transformed —becoming unfamiliar, and incapable of hiding his strong, violent emotions.*

12. "'Yes, forgotten by all else, but not by us. We dug the grave, and the polypi undertake to seal our dead for eternity.' And burying his face quickly in his hands, he tried in vain to suppress a sob."
(Part 1, Chapter 23, Page 114)

The Nautilus *crew, along with Professor Aronnax, Ned, and Conseil, attend a funeral for a slain member of the ship. Professor Aronnax does not know the details surrounding his death from a head injury. After the subterranean funeral, Captain Nemo is solemn and unable to contain his sadness, revealing another instance where control over his emotions slips. Professor Aronnax is increasingly seeing more sides to Captain Nemo.*

13. "This munificent charity from the man of the waters to the poor Cingalese was accepted with a trembling hand. His wondering eyes showed that he knew not what superhuman beings he owed both fortune and life."
(Part 2, Chapter 3, Page 130)

Captain Nemo attacks a shark when it tries to kill a lone fisherman. He stabs at the shark, unable to kill it until Ned Land strikes it with his harpoon. Captain Nemo then grabs the fisherman and brings him back to his boat. After Captain Nemo and Conseil revive him, Captain Nemo hands him a bag of pearls. The man accepts them with a shaking hand, unsure of what to make of the strange crew surrounding him in copper helmets. Captain Nemo has not only saved him, but bestowed a fortune of pearls upon him. It shows Professor Aronnax that Captain Nemo is not only brave and daring, but also capable of great acts of kindness.

14. "Thus the communication between the two was proved. I then sought for it with my *Nautilus,* I discovered it, ventured into it, and before long, sir, you too will have passed through my Arabian tunnel!"
(Part 2, Chapter 4, Page 139)

Captain Nemo has discovered a new route between the Red Sea and the Mediterranean—rather than taking the fastest and most direct route, the Suez Canal, they will travel via a subterranean route under the isthmus that Nemo has named the Arabian Tunnel. Nemo theorized that it existed, and proved it by putting gold rings on the tails of fish in the Red Sea. Six months later, those same fish appeared in the Mediterranean—another example of Captain Nemo's ingenuity.

15. "It was plain to me that this Mediterranean, enclosed in the midst of those countries which he wished to avoid, was distasteful to Captain Nemo. Those waves and those breezes brought back too many remembrances, if not too many regrets. Here he had no longer that independence and that liberty of gait which he had when in the open seas, and his *Nautilus* felt itself cramped between the close shores of Africa and Europe."

(Part 2, Chapter 7, Page 152)

When they reach the Mediterranean Sea, Professor Aronnax observes that Captain Nemo avoids making an appearance and determines that the area most likely brings back bad memories and regrets. Captain Nemo's more relaxed, independent nature is temporarily absent, and the vibe on the ship changes as a result. It feels more claustrophobic, especially since the ship mainly stays under the surface of the water.

16. "But I had guessed that whatever the motive which had forced him to seek independence under the sea, it had left him still a man, that his heart still beat for the sufferings of humanity, and that his immense charity was for oppressed races as well as individuals."
(Part 2, Chapter 8, Page 162)

When discussing the vast submarine treasure Captain Nemo is collecting in Vigo Bay, Professor Aronnax says he regrets that unfortunate people will be deprived of its riches. Captain Nemo immediately defends gathering the treasure, explaining that he has sympathy for oppressed people and is not ignorant of human suffering. Professor Aronnax realizes that although Captain Nemo has taken a life of isolation at sea, he still thinks about the plight of other people and provides generously for those who need it.

17. "I followed him with unshaken confidence. He seemed to me like a genie of the sea; and, as he walked before me, I could not help admiring his stature, which was outlined in black on the luminous horizon."
(Part 2, Chapter 9, Page 165)

Captain Nemo takes Professor Aronnax on a late-night excursion to the lost ruins of Atlantis. Even though they must walk in the dark water with only a light in the distance to guide them, Professor Aronnax follows Captain Nemo without hesitation. As he follows Captain Nemo, he feels admiration for the man who fearlessly guides him—comparing him to a magical genie. He knows that Captain Nemo has never wavered in his confidence navigating the often-dangerous aquatic realms around them.

18. "For a man unaccustomed to walk on land, the Captain climbed the steep slopes with an agility I never saw equaled, and which a hunter would have envied."
(Part 2, Chapter 14, Page 198)

Professor Aronnax follows Captain Nemo up to the summit of a peak in order to determine if they are in the South Pole. Professor Aronnax is amazed that a man who rarely walks on land is so agile, possessing a quickness of step that is unrivaled. He is able to climb with an ease that would make many hunters jealous.

19. "The situation was terrible. But every one had looked danger in the face, and each was determined to do his duty to the last."
(Part 2, Chapter 16, Page 205)

In the South Pole, the Nautilus is trapped, surrounded by ice sheets on all sides. The air supply is limited. Every man on the ship becomes a part of the effort to free it from its ice prison. They know their lives are at stake, and they are willing to do whatever it takes to survive. Even Ned Land commits himself to doing everything possible to get them out of the ice.

20. "But Captain Nemo was before me; his axe disappeared between the two enormous jaws, and miraculously saved the Canadian, rising, plunged his harpoon deep into the triple heart of the poulp."
(Part 2, Chapter 18, Page 222)

Near the Bahamas, the ship is attacked by roughly a dozen giant squids with huge tentacles and mouths like beaks. The men rush out to fight them, including Professor Aronnax, Ned, Conseil, and Captain Nemo. When one throws Ned to the ground and nearly eats him, Captain Nemo comes to his rescue by striking at the creature's jaws with his ax. Although Ned has been eager to leave the ship, he joins the fight when the creatures attack. He is then rescued by the man he has long wanted to get away from. He recognizes Captain Nemo's heroic act by silently bowing to him.

21. "The Canadian was evidently losing all patience. His vigorous nature could not stand this prolonged imprisonment. His face altered daily; his temper became more surly. I knew what he must suffer, for I was seized with nostalgia myself. Nearly seven months had passed without our having had any news from land. Captain Nemo's isolation, his altered spirits, especially since the fight with the poulps, his taciturnity, all made me view things in a different light."
(Part 2, Chapter 21, Pages 224 - 225)

Ned, a man who needs his freedom, has long been tired of the Nautilus, *and Professor Aronnax increasingly understands and sympathizes with his position. Captain Nemo's dark side has changed Aronnax's view of a man he at first admired and respected. Professor Aronnax knows his loyalties ultimately lie with Ned and Conseil, and Ned's growing impatience brings a greater sense of urgency to their plans to escape.*

22. "I turned to Captain Nemo. That terrible avenger, a perfect archangel of hatred, was still looking."
(Part 2, Chapter 21, Page 238)

Captain Nemo attacks the vessel that's been firing on them, claiming it's the reason he's lost everything, including his family. He runs the spur of the Nautilus *into the other ship. When Professor Aronnax finds Captain Nemo in the saloon, he's watching the ship sink, its men struggling in the water. Although Aronnax once admired Captain Nemo, he now sees him as a man embodying only hatred and vengeance. He finds it shocking that Captain Nemo simply looks on as other men die. It is a side of him that Professor Aronnax has been increasingly exposed to, and now knows is one of his defining qualities.*

23. "At that moment, I heard the distant strains of the organ, a sad harmony to an undefinable chant, the wail of a soul longing to break these earthly bonds. I listened with every sense, scarcely breathing, plunged, like Captain Nemo, in that musical ecstasy which was drawing him in spirit to the end of life."
(Part 2, Chapter 22, Page 241)

As Professor Aronnax is sneaking out to escape the Nautilus, *he hears Captain Nemo playing the organ in the saloon. The melancholy sounds are a reflection of Captain Nemo's darkened state. Professor Aronnax is entranced, listening intently. The music emanating from Captain Nemo seems to beckon him to his final moments, which are inevitable as the ship heads into a deadly whirlpool. The moment reveals the tragic turn Captain Nemo's journey has taken. Although he once held the admiration of Professor Aronnax, he is now defined entirely by his rage and despair.*

24. "We were in dread. Our horror was at its height, circulation had stopped, all nervous influence was annihilated, and we were covered with cold sweat, like a sweat of agony! And what noise around our frail bark! What roarings repeated by the echo miles away!"

(Part 2, Chapter 22, Page 243)

In their attempt to escape, Professor Aronnax, Ned, and Conseil head toward the giant maelstrom, along with the Nautilus, *to which they are still attached. They are seized with fear, their cries drowned out by the sounds of roaring waves crashing into the sharp rocks below. It is the moment that will decide their fate: whether they will break free from the* Nautilus *or find themselves tethered to it forever as it goes down into the massive whirlpool.*

25. "And I also hope that his powerful vessel has conquered the sea at its most terrible gulf, and that the *Nautilus* has survived where so many other vessels have been lost! If it be so—if Captain Nemo still inhabits the ocean, his adopted country, may hatred be appeased in that savage heart! May the contemplation of so many wonders extinguish for ever the spirit of vengeance!"
(Part 2, Chapter 23, Page 244)

Although Professor Aronnax, Ned, and Conseil survive the maelstrom, the fate of Captain Nemo is unknown. Professor Aronnax hopes the man that showed him the mysteries of the sea has survived that which has destroyed so many others, and continued on his journey. He also hopes that his heart is no longer filled with rage, and is instead lighted by curiosity and wonder inspired by the depths of the sea. Professor Aronnax has been deeply moved by his adventures, and wants the same for Captain Nemo. The two men carry a permanent bond in their unique knowledge of the secrets of the ocean's depths.

Essay Topics

1. Why does Professor Aronnax find Captain Nemo so captivating and worthy of admiration? What luxuries and privileges does being aboard the *Nautilus* give Aronnax? How do they shape his view of Captain Nemo?

2. Does keeping so much of Captain Nemo a mystery add to or take away from the novel? How does it affect the reader's impression of this character?

3. Research some of the real-life inventions Verne puts into his fictional world. How does this blending of fact and imagination define the genre of science fiction Verne created?

4. Are there disadvantages to Captain Nemo's technological prowess? Explain your answer using examples.

5. Using examples, discuss how the underwater environment is portrayed in the book. What is the world beneath the sea like? How does it compare to the world on land?

6. Compare Captain Nemo to the real-life explorers Verne references in the novel. How does his view of what he explores differ from theirs? How is it the same?

7. Why has Captain Nemo rejected humanity? What actions does he take to support his feelings? What actions does he take to complicate them?

8. Does Captain Nemo's character change during Professor Aronnax's time on the *Nautilus*? Or is Professor Aronnax simply more aware of qualities he ignored in the beginning? Use evidence to support your

answer.

9. Compare the novel's leaders. What are the power dynamics between Captain Nemo and his crew, Professor Aronnax and Conseil, and Captain Farragut and his ship? What does the novel say about leadership?

10. Discuss the novel's ending. Is it satisfying not to know Captain Nemo's fate? How does not knowing what happens to Nemo affect Professor Aronnax?

Made in the USA
Thornton, CO
04/28/22 08:48:57

03d1c629-dd7a-49b3-b471-04bc89805a33R03